Jesus according to the New Testament

Jesus according to the New Testament

James D. G. Dunn

William B. Eerdmans Publishing Company
Grand Rapids, Michigan

Wm. B. Eerdmans Publishing Co.
4035 Park East Court SE, Grand Rapids, Michigan 49546
www.eerdmans.com

28 27 26 25 24 23 22 21 20 19   2 3 4 5 6 7 8 9 10

ISBN 978-0-8028-7669-0

Library of Congress Cataloging-in-Publication Data

Names: Dunn, James D. G., 1939- author.
Title: Jesus according to the New Testament / James D. G. Dunn.
Description: Grand Rapids : Eerdmans Publishing Co., 2019. |
    Includes bibliographical references and index.
Identifiers: LCCN 2018024862 | ISBN 9780802876690 (pbk. : alk. paper)
Subjects: LCSH: Jesus Christ.—Person and offices—Biblical teaching. |
    Bible. New Testament—Criticism, interpretation, etc.
Classification: LCC BT203 .D859 2019 | DDC 232—dc23
    LC record available at https://lccn.loc.gov/2018024862

For St. Paul's Church,
Chichester, and the Chichester Diocese

Contents

CONTENTS

Foreword

Readers of the New Testament in Christian congregations (and among a wider public too) are quite likely these days to feel a certain amount of bewilderment at the variety and complexity of what is written on the subject. Those who venture a little into the scholarly literature, as well as those who pick up the latest sensational stories in the media about "lost" gospels and alternative histories, may feel like echoing Mary Magdalene: "They have taken away my Lord, and I do not know where they have laid him." What do we—what *can* we—really know about Jesus? Is the New Testament just the deposit of a confused mass of unreliable traditions, put together under the iron hand of a narrow church authority?

Professor Dunn, one of the most respected and prolific biblical scholars of our time, with a long string of innovative, comprehensive studies of the New Testament text to his name, begins with a simple but all-important question in this book. It is really a commonsensical one: What must have been going on in the life, and indeed in the mind, of Jesus for any of the New Testament texts to have been *possible*? To ask such a question does not mean that everything we read in the New Testament is a straightforward record of events or that the ideas of the first believers are immediately accessible to us. But it does remind us that the movement whose writings we read in the canonical Gospels, Acts, and letters began with the narrative of a specific historical figure whose words and actions were sufficiently different from the norm to attract attention.

Like some other scholars in recent years, Professor Dunn is skeptical about the skepticism that has prevailed in a fair amount of learned discussion. If certain things had not been true about Jesus, it is simply very hard to see how certain kinds of text and certain kinds of talk would ever have emerged. Many writers have stressed that there are aspects of the gospel stories that seem to be preserved even though the earliest churches did not fully understand them—like Jesus's description of himself as "Son of Man" or the whole way he is remembered as speaking about God's kingdom. If he never said a word about how he understood the death he knew he was risking, it would be hard to see why and how the quite dense and complicated language used to interpret baptism and the Lord's Supper got started. And—most simply of all, a point well brought out by Professor Dunn—Jesus was remembered as a storyteller in a way that is not true of any other figure in the New Testament and that is rare among his Jewish contemporaries. The parables are among the most plainly distinctive things in the traditions about Jesus, and they tell us something of his understanding of the relation between the everyday and the holy which is still radical.

The New Testament is tantalizing for readers because its texts are both startlingly different from one another and startlingly convergent. Just this mixture of difference and convergence is exactly what should make us pause before accepting the fashionable idea that what we have in the New Testament is some sort of unrepresentative selection of writings which just happened to be acceptable to dictatorial prelates in the early centuries. With exemplary clarity and understated scholarly acumen, Professor Dunn traces both the continuities between these diverse texts and the communities that used them, and the discontinuities, the local emphases and sometimes controversial new twists to the story that developed in some quarters. Many readers will find it liberating to realize that to believe in the consistency of the New Testament is not the same as having to suppose that every writer says the same thing. From the very first, what happens in and around the figure of Jesus is experienced as too immense to be communicated in one telling, seen from one perspective; as the end of John's Gospel already says so eloquently, the world could not contain all that would need to be said.

So this survey of what the story of Jesus meant in the first Christian generations becomes a powerful theological testimony to the scale of the mystery laid bare in those events. This is a book that will nurture a faith that is not uncritical but is also being directed constantly back toward the wonder of the first witnesses. It is as we make that wonder our own that our faith grows and deepens; Professor Dunn helps us toward that enrichment of joy, trust, and gratitude.

ROWAN WILLIAMS

Preface

The Diocese of Chichester, in south coast England, some years ago launched a splendid tradition. It began with the intention of preparing the diocese for the Gospel of the year—first Matthew, then Mark, and then Luke. Somewhat oddly, I thought, John was never the Gospel for the year. So in Chichester we broke with the tradition after the third year and turned first to John and then to Paul.

In 2015, I was invited to lecture in Canterbury, and the happy thought came to me that I could adapt my Chichester lectures for Canterbury. The obvious focal point was, of course, Jesus—the challenge being to sketch out the different ways in which Jesus was presented by the Gospel writers. With only three lecture slots to work with, and the first three Gospels (Matthew, Mark, and Luke) being so similar, it made sense to take them together, when their distinctive features could be brought out by close comparison. John was sufficiently distinctive in itself to be considered separately. That left free a third slot. And what could be better than to start by focusing on what we could know of the reports, memories, and traditions of Jesus and his ministry behind the Gospels?

And so emerged a sequence: Jesus according to . . . First, "Jesus according to Jesus," then "Jesus according to Mark, Matthew, and Luke," and finally "Jesus according to John." These lectures seemed to work well, bringing into sharper focus the distinctive features in each case, indicating how differently Jesus was remembered and his significance celebrated.

Then the thought arose: Why not continue the sequence, highlighting the different impacts Jesus made and the central role he filled in the writings that make up the New Testament? And so emerged "Jesus according to Acts," "Jesus according to Paul," and the rest. Some introduction was necessary in each case. But the old introductory questions that begin particular commentaries on the New Testament writings (Who wrote what, when, and where?) seemed to be for the most part unnecessary. After all, they usually do not much affect what we learn from the writings themselves. But they do help set the writings in their historical context, and thus also help us understand them better—especially when the historical situation helps explain features of the text that we might otherwise misunderstand. So I have added at the end an indication of where and when the writings are thought to come from (Appendix 1). That there is uncertainty in many cases should not detract from the recognition that the documents were written at particular times and to serve particular needs. Also indicated is the probable time line and historical context of Paul's mission and writing (Appendix 2), since he is the principal contributor to the New Testament and since we have a fuller idea of his mission and writings than that of any other New Testament author.

And then the further thought came: Why not continue on the same pathway? The story of Jesus and reactions to him hardly cease with the end of the New Testament. But to press forward into the second century and beyond, with chapters such as "Jesus according to Ignatius," "Jesus according to Augustine," "Jesus according to Luther," would extend the project into two or more volumes. And I had to admit that I lacked the knowledge about such historic writers on Jesus to do them justice. I also wondered about a final chapter with contributions from friends in our local church adding their own brief testimonies, including my own testimony, "Jesus according to Me." But to slot our own brief pieces alongside those of the New Testament writers began to seem rather vainglorious. So I let that idea slip away too, not without regret.

Nevertheless, if the present volume has any appeal, there is no reason why other volumes should not follow, with someone else better equipped than me to draw out the testimony of Christian greats through the centuries. And no reason why a(nother) volume of brief testimonies from disciples of today should not follow. After all, everything we know about Jesus is thanks to the personal testimony of his most immediate followers. But for Christians, Jesus is not just a figure of the past. Christians today are disciples of the present. So why not continue the story of Jesus up to the present, with everyday believers bearing witness to what attracts or intrigues them about Jesus? How about it?

CHAPTER ONE

Jesus according to

Jesus

C an we be confident that we are able to get back to Jesus's
own message and views of himself? John Meier certainly
has no doubts on the subject—and the five volumes of *A
Marginal Jew: Rethinking the Historical Jesus* include a clear and
fully worked-out answer.[1] Perhaps, however, a briefer answer will
help focus attention on the key features that enable us to speak
with confidence not only of the impact that Jesus made but also
of Jesus's own understanding of what he was about. The obvious
way to go about it is to focus on the distinctive features of what the
first Christians remembered about Jesus as recorded by the earliest evangelists.[2] The following pages explore this in three ways:
lessons learned from Jesus, distinctive features of Jesus's ministry,
and Jesus's own self-understanding.[3]

1. John P. Meier, *A Marginal Jew: Rethinking the Historical Jesus*, 5 vols. (New
Haven: Yale University Press, 1991–2016).

2. The writers of the Gospels are often referred to as "evangelists" ("evangel"
= "gospel").

3. I have restricted the footnotes to a minimum. For more detailed discussion, see James D. G. Dunn, *Jesus Remembered*, vol. 1 of *Christianity in the Making*
(Grand Rapids: Eerdmans, 2003). The content of this chapter has been adapted
from this earlier work.

Lessons Learned from Jesus

There are quite a number of emphases and priorities that we can say with some confidence the first followers of Jesus attributed to Jesus.

The Love Command

The summation of the love command is recorded by the first three Gospels.[4] Since all three agree on the principal features, we need cite only Mark's version:

> One of the scribes . . . asked him, "Which commandment is the first of all?" Jesus answered, "The first is, 'Hear, O Israel: the Lord our God, the Lord is one; and you shall love the Lord your God with all your heart. . . .' The second is this, 'You shall love your neighbor as yourself.' There is no other commandment greater than these." (Mark 12:28–31)[5]

The first quotation comes from Deuteronomy 6:5, the fundamental creed of Israel, so it would occasion no surprise to those who first heard and circulated the Jesus tradition. It is the second commandment that would be something of a surprise when first uttered. For it comes from a much less well-known and less-used passage in the Torah: Leviticus 19:18. In early Jewish reflection it is hardly as prominent as the first—the third clause in a verse that is part of a sequence regarding personal relationships and obligations. "You shall not hate in your heart anyone of your kin; you shall reprove your neighbor, or you will incur guilt yourself. You shall not take vengeance or bear a grudge against any of your people, but you shall love your neighbor as yourself: I am the LORD" (Lev 19:17–18).

---

4. Mark 12:28–31 // Matt 22:35–40 // Luke 10:25–28.
5. Unless otherwise indicated, biblical quotations are either from the New Revised Standard Version or are the author's own translation.

Such esteem for Leviticus 19:18c as the second of the two commandments that sum up the law of God is exceptional. Explicit references to Leviticus 19:18 are lacking in Jewish literature prior to Jesus, and the allusions that exist give it no particular prominence—though, subsequently, the opinion is attributed to Rabbi Akiba (early second century CE) that Leviticus 19:18 is "the greatest general principle in the Torah."[6] Since the prominence given in the earliest history of Christianity to the command to "Love your neighbor as yourself"[7] is most obviously attributed to the influence of Jesus's teaching, it is probably not unfair to deduce that the similar emphasis of Akiba attests the same influence. At any rate, the abstraction and exaltation of Leviticus 19:18c as the second of the two greatest commandments can be confidently attributed to Jesus and strongly attests his influence.

Priority of the Poor

This priority is most striking in several Gospel passages. Notable is Jesus's response to the rich young man, who had observed all the commandments but lacked one thing: "Go, sell what you own, and give to the poor, and you will have treasure in heaven" (Mark 10:21 parr.). Similarly his commendation of the poor widow who in giving two copper coins to the treasury had, in Jesus's perspective, "out of her poverty . . . put in everything she had, all she had to live on" (Mark 12:42–44 // Luke 21:2–4). In Jesus's response to the Baptist's question as to whether he (Jesus) was the fulfillment of (messianic) expectation, the climax in Jesus's answer is that "the poor have good news brought to them" (Matt 11:5 // Luke 7:22). Notable too is the way Luke begins his account of Jesus's mission, by narrating Jesus's reading from Isaiah 61 in the Nazareth synagogue: "The Spirit of the Lord is upon me, because he has anointed me to preach good news to the poor" (Luke 4:18). And

---

6. Sifra on Lev 19:18.
7. Rom 13:8–10; Gal 5:14; Jas 2:8; Didache 1:2; 2:7; Barnabas 19:5; Gospel of Thomas 25.

equally striking is Luke's version of the Beatitudes—the first being "Blessed are you who are poor, for yours is the kingdom of God" (Luke 6:20; an interesting variation of the version in Matthew: "Blessed are the poor in spirit" [Matt 5:3]). It should occasion little surprise, then, that for Luke a key feature of the gospel is that it is good news for the poor: that it is the poor, the maimed, the lame, and the blind who should be invited to a great feast (Luke 14:13, 21); and Zacchaeus demonstrates his readiness for salvation in that he gives half of his goods to the poor (Luke 19:8).

Of course, the priority of the poor is a prominent emphasis within Israel's own law (e.g., Deut 15:11). But that the particular concern for the poor so prominent among the first Christians is to be attributed to the influence of Jesus's own emphasis can hardly be doubted. So with the early concern among disciples in the Jerusalem community for the poor widows among their members that resulted in the first formal Christian organization (Acts 6:1–6). The profound concern for the poor displayed by James attests the same concern (Jas 2:2–6). The same impression is given by the fact that in the Jerusalem agreement—that gentile converts need not be circumcised—the only other concern indicated was "that we remember the poor, which," Paul adds, "was actually what I was eager to do" (Gal 2:10). Similarly there can be little doubt as to why Paul gave such importance to helping the poor among the saints in Jerusalem, making a special collection for them in the churches that he had founded, and was willing to risk his own life to bring the collection to Jerusalem.[8] We may be confident, then, that concern for the poor is one of the priorities that the first Christians learned from Jesus.

Sinners Welcome

A particular feature of Jesus's ministry that caused surprise and shock to his religious contemporaries was his openness to those regarded as unacceptable in religious company. According to the

---

8. Rom 15:25–31; 2 Cor 8–9.

first three Gospels, it was one of the features of Jesus's conduct that drew criticism from the "righteous." Early in his account Mark reports the offense Jesus caused by his readiness to eat "with sinners and tax collectors." "Why does he do this?" complained Pharisees and scribes. To which Jesus famously replied, "Those who are well have no need of a physician, but those who are sick; I have come to call not the righteous but sinners" (Luke adds ". . . to repentance"; Mark 2:16–17 parr.). Matthew and Luke (Q)[9] note a similar criticism later: "Look, a glutton and a drunkard, a friend of tax collectors and sinners!" (Matt 11:19 // Luke 7:34). But it is again Luke who gives particular emphasis to this aspect of Jesus's conduct. He notes the repeated criticism of Jesus on this point: "This fellow welcomes sinners and eats with them" (Luke 15:2). To which Jesus replies with the parables of the shepherd's lost sheep and the woman's lost silver coin: that of course the shepherd goes in search of the sheep and the woman for the coin until they find what had been lost (Luke 15:3–10). Luke alone narrates the parable contrasting the prayers of the Pharisee and the tax collector, in which it is the latter who prays, "God, be merciful to me a sinner," whose prayer is truly heard (Luke 18:9–14). And it is Luke alone who narrates the episode in which Jesus goes to be a guest with the "chief tax collector," Zacchaeus, despite the criticism that Zacchaeus was "a sinner." The episode ends with Jesus's reassurance that salvation has come to this house, since he (Zacchaeus) also is a son of Abraham (Luke 19:1–10).

It is hardly surprising, then, that Paul could sum up the gospel in terms of the great reversal—of God's love for *sinners*. "God proves his love for us in that while we still were sinners Christ died for us" (Rom 5:8). "For just as by the one man's disobedience the many were made sinners, so by the one man's obedience the many will be made righteous" (Rom 5:19). And it was Paul who pressed the logic of the gospel: that if gentiles are to be classified as "sinners," then, of course, the gospel is for them too, justification being by faith in Christ and not by doing the works of the law (Gal

9. Q is one of the sources on which Matthew and Luke drew. For more on Q, see chapter 2.

2:15–17). It can hardly be doubted that this extension of the gospel, to gentiles as well as Jews, was the direct result of the recognition that the good news that Jesus brought was primarily for sinners.

Openness to Gentiles

Jesus's commission of his disciples, in effect to join in his ministry, raises the question whether Jesus himself was open to gentiles: "Go nowhere among the Gentiles, and enter no town of the Samaritans, but go rather to the lost sheep of the house of Israel" (Matt 10:5–6). But Matthew records this as in effect simply a (preliminary) phase in Jesus's ministry, since he takes more pains to emphasize that Jesus saw the gospel as for gentiles also. It is Matthew alone who provides Isaiah 42:1–4 as one of the Old Testament prophecies that Jesus fulfilled, climaxing in the expectation that "in his [Christ's] name the Gentiles will hope" (Matt 12:21). It is Matthew who adds to the account of the healing of the centurion's servant the prediction of Jesus that "many will come from east and west and will eat with Abraham and Isaac and Jacob in the kingdom of heaven, while the heirs of the kingdom will be thrown into the outer darkness" (Matt 8:11–12). And it is Matthew who ends his Gospel with Jesus commissioning the apostles to "Go therefore and make disciples of all nations" (Matt 28:19). So we can be confident that Matthew was fully in accord with the early Christian conviction that the gospel was also for gentiles and that this conviction was fully in accord with Jesus and with his preaching and expectation during his earthly ministry.[10]

Women among His Close Followers

Somewhat oddly Mark concludes his account of Jesus's crucifixion and death by noting that on the edge of the onlookers were

---

10. The equivalent passage in John's Gospel is John 12:20–26, though the point is not so clearly made.

women, Mary Magdalene, Mary the mother of James the younger and of Joses, and Salome, who had followed and ministered to him in Galilee, and also "many other women who had come up with him to Jerusalem" (Mark 15:40–41).[11] The oddity, of course, includes the fact that precisely at this point Jesus's male disciples seem to have abandoned Jesus altogether—though John adds that "the disciple whom Jesus loved" was there with the women (John 19:25–27). Luke and John earlier both tell the touching story of Jesus's closeness to the sisters Martha and Mary (Luke 10:38–42; John 11). And Matthew and John make special mention of initial resurrection appearances to Mary Magdalene in particular at Jesus's now empty tomb.[12] The fact that none of these appearances are included in what we may regard as the formal list of resurrection appearances drawn on by Paul in 1 Corinthians 15:3–8 is presumably just a reminder that women's testimony was not given as much weight as men's. It is all the more notable, therefore, that, despite what was regarded as the weaker status of women's testimony, Matthew and John nevertheless give prominence to the appearances to Mary Magdalene in particular.

That this testimony would have been regarded as shocking to Jesus's contemporaries may well have been a factor in ensuring that the testimony was preserved and given expression in the written Gospels—a reminder that women were an important part of Jesus's disciple group and played a vital role within it. And should we not see a connection here with the prominence of women among Paul's coworkers? That the ex-Pharisee, previously committed to the maintenance of Jewish tradition, including the lower status of women, should after his conversion include many women among his close colleagues and "coworkers," a little over 20 percent,[13] should probably be regarded as an indication of the often unmentioned influence of the tradition of Jesus's ministry on Paul.

11. The parallels in Matthew and Luke are not so full (Matt 27:55–56 and Luke 23:49).

12. Matt 27:55–56; John 20:11–18.

13. See James D. G. Dunn, *Beginning from Jerusalem*, vol. 2 of *Christianity in the Making* (Grand Rapids: Eerdmans, 2009), 571.

Openness to Children

The key incident recollected by the first three Gospels is Mark 10:13–16 parr. Notable is the fact, recorded by all three evangelists, that when people brought children to Jesus, that he might bless the children, his disciples rebuked them. Jesus's own indignant response was, "Let the children come to me; do not stop them; for it is to such as these that the kingdom of God belongs" (Mark 10:14). Mark and Luke add Jesus's saying, "Truly I tell you, whoever does not receive the kingdom of God as a little child will never enter it" (Mark 10:15 // Luke 18:17).[14] Given the notable influence of Jesus on the personal relations of his disciples, we should probably detect the influence of Jesus here too in the "household codes" that appear in the later Pauline letters.[15] Such household codes were familiar then, but notable in Paul's exhortations is the assumption that children and slaves would be fully part of the Christian gathering and could or should be addressed directly. It is hardly straining the evidence to infer that this too attests the continuing influence of Jesus's mission on his disciples.

Relaxation of Food Laws

This is one of the most remarkable features of Jesus's mission, not least since it cut so sharply across a traditional Jewish concern for purity. Not surprisingly it is given extensive treatment by Mark and Matthew (Mark 7:1–23 // Matt 15:1–20). It begins with some Pharisees' criticism that Jesus's disciples "ate with hands defiled, that is, unwashed." The Greek word used here (*koinos* = "common") reflects the distinctively Jewish sense of "profane, unclean, defiled."[16] Jesus responds by citing Isaiah 29:13: "This people honors me with their lips, but their hearts are far from me; in vain do they worship me, teaching human precepts as doctrines." And from that

14. Matthew includes a variation of the saying earlier (Matt 18:3).
15. Eph 6:1–9; Col 3:18–4:1.
16. Dunn, *Jesus Remembered*, 571n123.

he draws the highly critical conclusion: "You abandon the commandment of God and hold to human tradition" (Mark 7:6–8).

The Jesus tradition continues in both Mark and Matthew, by further challenging the traditional Jewish concept of purity (Matt 15:10–20 // Mark 7:14–23). The Matthean version of the tradition is content to draw a sharp comparison between inner and outer purity: "It is not what goes into the mouth that defiles a person, but it is what comes out of the mouth that defiles" (Matt 15:11).[17] But in Mark the teaching is sharper: "There is nothing outside a person that by going in can defile, but the things that come out are what defile [a person]" (Mark 7:15). And in the following explanation that Jesus gives, it is clear that Jesus is remembered as teaching that what goes into a person cannot defile the person. Mark makes the point clear by adding, "Thus he declared all foods clean" (Mark 7:18–19).

We know from Paul that the issue of clean and unclean foods came alive in the wider gentile mission. The issue there was whether Jesus's followers could eat meat that had been sacrificed to idols (the most common supply of food in the ancient meat markets).[18] Paul's advice was clear: "Nothing is unclean in itself; but it is unclean for anyone who thinks it unclean" (Rom 14:14). What is intriguing is that Mark's version of Jesus's teaching on the subject of food purity seems to reflect the strong affirmation of Paul. In other words, it is in this teaching in particular that we can see the influence of Jesus's priorities being further reflected on by Paul, and the inferences drawn from his teaching being reflected back into the memory of his teaching.

The Last Supper or Lord's Supper

Finally, in recounting what Christianity learned from Jesus, we should not forget the centrality in the first Christians' memory

---

17. Matthew and Luke (Q) also recall Jesus rebuking Pharisees for counting outward cleanliness as more important than inward cleanliness (Matt 23:25–26 // Luke 11:39–41).

18. Rom 14:1–15:6; 1 Cor 8–10.

and practice of Jesus's last meal with his disciples before his death. The first three Gospels make plain how important that special time with Jesus was for his disciples (Mark 14:22–25 parr.). We do not know how frequently the Lord's Supper was celebrated in the earliest decades of Christianity. But Paul makes it equally clear that the shared meal, beginning with the shared bread ("This is my body that is broken for you") and ending with the shared cup ("This cup is the new covenant in my blood"), was explicitly remembered as a sacred memory initiated by Jesus himself (1 Cor 11:23–26). It sums up as nothing else does that Christianity is deeply rooted in Jesus's own ministry climaxing in his death.

It is striking, then, how much of what was important for the first Christians can be traced back directly to the influence of Jesus's own ministry and teaching.

Distinctive Features of Jesus's Ministry

For much or indeed most of the twentieth century, primary attention in scholarship on Jesus was given to what the first Christians thought about Jesus. Surprisingly little attention or concern was devoted to the impact made by Jesus himself, to such an extent that it could easily be concluded that little can now be discerned of the historical Jesus and his teaching. But the probability that Jesus made an impact on his first disciples, and that this impact is clearly indicated in the Jesus tradition, is such an obvious starting point that any scholarship that denies our ability to speak with credibility of the teaching and ministry of Jesus would seem to be unduly skeptical and prejudiced. We have already noted how much in earliest Christianity can be attributed with confidence to the influence of Jesus's conduct and teaching. Now it can be added that not least of significance is the fact that there are distinctive features of Jesus's ministry that stand out in the accounts of Jesus's ministry and that cannot plausibly be said to have originated in later evaluations of his ministry.

The Kingdom of God

When we read the first three Gospels, it is easy and quite natural to conclude that proclamation of the kingdom of God was the principal feature of Jesus's preaching. Mark introduces and sums up Jesus's preaching in precisely these terms: "The time is fulfilled, and the kingdom of God has come near; repent, and believe in the good news" (Mark 1:15). Matthew and Luke both summarize Jesus's preaching in the same terms: Jesus "went throughout Galilee . . . proclaiming the gospel of the kingdom" (Matt 4:23). Jesus said to his disciples, "I must proclaim the good news of the kingdom of God to the other cities also" (Luke 4:43). When Jesus sent out his disciples in mission, it was to proclaim the same message: "The kingdom of heaven has come near" (Matt 10:7 // Luke 10:9). A notable example of his kingdom preaching is the first item of Jesus's beatitudes or blessings: "Blessed are you who are poor, for yours is the kingdom of God" (Luke 6:20 // Matt 5:3). Also prominent is Jesus's claim that his healing ministry was itself a manifestation of the kingdom: "If it is by the Spirit of God that I cast out demons, then the kingdom of God has come to you" (Matt 12:28 // Luke 11:20). And notable too are Jesus's kingdom parables: for example, "[The kingdom of God] is like a mustard seed" (Mark 4:31 parr.).

It is easy to see, then, that Jesus's preaching ministry can be summed up in terms of his proclamation of the kingdom of God, not only imminent but already in evidence in his ministry. The kingdom of God (or, of heaven, in Matthew's preferred version) is mentioned more than fifty times in the tradition shared by the first three written Gospels. This makes it all the more astonishing that references to the kingdom of God thereafter are so thin. For example, Paul picks up the theme of inheriting the kingdom of God,[19] but the thought of the kingdom as present and active is hardly a strong feature of his gospel, as it was of Jesus's ministry.[20] And, astonishingly when compared with the other Gospels,

19. 1 Cor 6:9; 15:10; Gal 5:21; Eph 5:5.
20. Rom 14:17; 1 Cor 4:20; Col 1:13.

the Gospel of John has Jesus referring to God's kingdom in only one pericope (John 3:3, 5), though John also includes Jesus referring to "my kingdom" in his trial before Pilate (John 18:36). The evidence, then, indicates that it is highly unlikely that memory and reworking of the Jesus tradition picked up the emphasis on the kingdom of God from later Christian interest in the theme. It is much more likely that Jesus's emphasis on the kingdom of God was slackened among his followers thereafter, presumably because in a Roman Empire alive to threats against its authority, promotion of any other kingdom could be presented as such a threat. Jesus's proclamation of God's kingdom was not a theme to be elaborated in Caesar's empire.

Teacher

Teacher is the most common title used for Jesus in the Jesus tradition—occurring nearly fifty times. The parallel between Jesus and his disciples on the one hand and rabbis and their pupils on the other hand is only partial, but the very fact that the immediate followers of Jesus were known as "disciples" (*mathētēs*, from *manthanein*, "to learn") certainly implies that Jesus was widely recognized as a teacher whose disciples followed him in order to learn.[21] Indeed, it is remembered that Jesus was occasionally addressed as "Rabbi" or "Rabbouni,"[22] and Matthew recalls that Jesus himself saw his relationship with his disciples in these terms (Matt 10:24–25 // Luke 6:40).

One of the features remembered about his teaching was the surprising authority with which he taught. He is recalled as one who provoked surprise and questioning concerning the authority of his teaching. For example, Mark characteristically links Jesus's teaching with his exorcisms and mighty works: "What is this? A

21. *Mathētēs* (disciple) is used frequently in the Gospels—seventy-three times in Matthew, forty-six times in Mark, thirty-seven times in Luke, and seventy-eight times in John.

22. Mark 9:5; 10:51; 11:21; 14:45; Matt 26:25; John 1:38, 49; 3:2; 4:31; 6:25; 9:2; 11:8.

new teaching—with authority! He commands even the unclean spirits and they obey him" (Mark 1:27). "Where did this man get all this? What is this wisdom that has been given to him? What deeds of power are being done by his hands!" (Mark 6:2). The high priestly delegation asked him, "By what authority are you doing these things? Who gave you this authority?" (Mark 11:28 parr.). Such surprise, even incredulity, is understandable given the presumably well-enough-known fact that Jesus lacked any formal training. It is all the more striking, then, that this emphasis on Jesus as a teacher is not retained among the earliest churches. Of course, Jesus was remembered as far more than a teacher in the earliest churches. But that very fact makes it all the less credible to argue that the references to Jesus as "teacher" were read back into the Jesus tradition. The fact that Jesus was widely known as a teacher during his ministry is one of the most firmly established features of the Jesus tradition.

Teaching by Parable

It was also one of the most distinctive features of Jesus's ministry that he was a parabolist. Stories, illustrations, or parables were not regular features of passing on traditional teaching within Judaism. So it is rather striking that Mark, at the end of his parable collection (Mark 4:1-32), sums up his portrayal of Jesus in these terms: "With many such parables he spoke the word to them, as they were able to hear it; he did not speak to them except in parables, but he explained everything in private to his disciples" (Mark 4:33-34 // Matt 13:34). Indeed, no fewer than forty-six parables are attributed to Jesus in the shared tradition—some featuring in all of the first three Gospels, like the sower (Mark 4:1-9, 13-20 parr.) and the wicked tenants (Mark 12:1-12 parr.); some probably in the tradition common to Matthew and Luke, like the parable of the talents (Matt 25:14-30 // Luke 19:11-27); some unique to Matthew, like the parables of the laborers in the vineyard (Matt 20:1-16) and the wise and foolish maidens (Matt 25:1-13); and over a third of the total distinctive of Luke, including some of the best known, such as the good Samaritan (Luke 10:25–37), the lost sheep, the lost coin, the lost son (Luke 15:1–32), the rich man and Lazarus (Luke 16:19–31), and the Pharisee and the tax collector (Luke 18:9–14). So the description of Jesus as a parabolist is well founded.

What is striking in comparison is that no one else among the disciples of Jesus or in the earliest churches is remembered as a parabolist. Paul, for example, is remembered for some vivid analogies, such as the olive tree with grafted branches (Rom 11:17–24), but he is hardly remembered as a parabolist. And, remarkably, John makes no effort to portray Jesus as a teller of parables; the "I am" sayings, particularly "I am the true vine" (John 15:1), are as near as he gets. So it would be very hard to maintain an argument that the portrayal of Jesus as a parabolist was anachronistically applied by the first Christians or the first three evangelists to the Jesus tradition. The only obvious explanation is that even if Jesus did not initiate a model of teaching followed by his disciples, we have to conclude at the very least that he was warmly remembered as one who typically taught by telling parables and that his parables made a lasting impression on his disciples.

Exorcising Evil Spirits

Exorcism was evidently one of the most prominent features of Jesus's ministry. We may note, for example, the accusation leveled against Jesus that he cast out demons "by the ruler of the demons" (Mark 3:22 parr.). To which Jesus responded: "How can Satan cast out Satan? If a kingdom is divided against itself, that kingdom cannot stand. And if a house is divided against itself, that house will not be able to stand. And if Satan has risen up against himself and is divided, he cannot stand, but his end has come. But no one can enter a strong man's house and plunder his property without first tying up the strong man; then indeed the house can be plundered" (Mark 3:23–27 parr.).

At this point Matthew and Luke insert a passage from their shared source appropriately: "If I cast out demons by Beelzebul, by whom do your sons cast them out? Therefore they shall be your judges. But if it is by the Spirit of God that I cast out demons, then the kingdom of God has come to you" (Matt 12:27–28 // Luke 11:19–20). It is evident, then, that Jesus was widely regarded as an exorcist.[23]

According to the first three evangelists, Jesus also commissioned his disciples to preach and to cast out demons.[24] And, quite unexpectedly,[25] when thus sent out, they seem to have been as successful as Jesus himself (Luke 10:17). It is somewhat surprising, then, that exorcism does not feature at all in the earliest churches. The term *daimonion* ("daemon" or "evil spirit") occurs sixty-seven times in the tradition shared by Mark, Matthew, and Luke, but only six times in John, and occasionally thereafter; but exorcisms as such are never mentioned again.[26] Casting out demons was evidently not a ministry that the first Christians exercised, despite having Jesus himself as their precedent. And if they did, they evidently did not think it worth recording. Either way, it is incredible to infer that Jesus's ministry as an exorcist was entirely read back into the Jesus tradition. Here too we can be confident that Jesus was known and remembered as a successful exorcist.

Concentration on Galilee

One of the curiosities that any comparison of the Gospel of John with the first three Gospels can hardly miss is that so much of John's account of Jesus's ministry is set in the south, in Judea and Jerusalem. In Mark, Matthew, and Luke the story of Jesus's ministry is clear. He was baptized by the Baptist in Judea. But after John was arrested and imprisoned, Jesus withdrew to the north,

---

23. Matt 9:32–34; 17:18; Mark 1:34, 39; 7:26–30; Luke 4:33–35, 41; 8:27–38; 9:42; 11:14–15; 13:32.

24. Mark 3:15; 6:7–13 parr.

25. Cf. Mark 9:18 parr.

26. Outside the first three Gospels, curing someone possessed by an "unclean spirit," as an alternative expression, appears only in Acts 5:16 and 8:7.

to Galilee (Mark 1:14 parr.). And there he ministered for the bulk of his ministry. It was only after Peter's confession of Jesus as the Messiah,[27] says Matthew, that Jesus "began to show his disciples that he must go to Jerusalem and undergo great suffering" there (Matt 16:21). Luke tells the same story: "When the days drew near for him to be taken up, he set his face to go to Jerusalem" (Luke 9:51). And it is generally recognized that the passion narrative begins with Jesus's entry into Jerusalem (Mark 11:1–10 parr.).

In contrast, John has Jesus going up to Jerusalem several times in the course of his ministry. John portrays Jesus as "cleansing the temple" early on (John 2:13–22), followed by his conversation with Nicodemus while he is still in Jerusalem (John 2:23–3:10). Jesus lingers in Judea and ministers effectively in Samaria (John 3:22–4:42), followed by an apparently brief spell in Galilee (John 4:43–54). In chapter 5 he is once again in Jerusalem, but in chapter 6 he is rather abruptly back in Galilee for the great bread of life discourse. Shortly after that, however, he again goes up to Jerusalem (John 7:10), and, surprisingly, he never returns to Galilee thereafter. John in fact highlights the degree of surprise that his portrayal causes by mentioning the disbelief of the Jerusalem crowd that any good could come from Galilee (John 7:41, 52).

It is easy to see how the contrast between the first three Gospels and John came about. For whatever reason, Mark, who first composed a "gospel" (Mark 1:1), decided to focus on Jesus's ministry in Galilee and to portray his trip to Jerusalem, with his betrayal, crucifixion, and resurrection, as the climax. In this he was followed by Matthew and Luke, both using Mark as their template. John, however, suggests that Jesus in fact made earlier trips to Jerusalem, to take part in annual festivals, prior to his final journey climaxing in his passion. The issue is complicated by John's transfer of the cleansing of the temple episode to the beginning of Jesus's ministry, probably as a "sign" to indicate the character of his ministry (John 2:18–22). But that may simply remind us that John saw his attempt to bring out the significance of Jesus's mis-

---

27. "Messiah" (= *christos* in Greek) was the title of Israel's longed-for deliverer.

sion as different from and as less constrained by historical detail than the earlier evangelists. Either way, both bring out distinctives of Jesus's ministry as it was variously remembered.

Submission to High Priestly Authorities

We should simply note that Jesus was remembered as in effect willingly surrendering himself to the Jerusalem authorities. As we saw in the last section, the first three Gospels make Jesus's decision to go to Jerusalem the turning point in their respective tellings of the story of Jesus. Mark sets the scene by showing Jesus making a sequence of passion predictions in (what are now) successive chapters.[28] The third is the most explicit: "The Son of Man will be handed over to the chief priests and the scribes, and they will condemn him to death; then they will hand him over to the Gentiles; they will mock him, and spit upon him, and flog him, and kill him; and after three days he will rise again" (Mark 10:33–34).

What is striking, and can be listed as another distinctive of Jesus's ministry, is that Jesus is thus remembered as going willingly and knowingly to his betrayal and death in Jerusalem. This is in some contrast to his withdrawal from danger after Herod's execution of John the Baptist (Matt 14:13 parr.). The way in which the evangelists set out their accounts of the good news, beginning with the baptism by John, subsequently to be executed, and with early warning indications (such as Mark 3:6), shows that the characterization of the gospels as "passion narratives with an extended introduction"[29] faithfully represents a ministry that climaxed in submission to the Jerusalem authorities.

It is not difficult, then, to see these features as distinctive of Jesus's actual ministry—none of them first read back into the Jesus tradition at a subsequent date, but each of them truly remembered by his disciples, having made a lasting impact on

28. Mark 8:31; 9:31; 10:33–34.
29. See the discussion of Martin Kähler in the next chapter.

them, and providing core features of their retelling of the story of that ministry.

Jesus's Self-Understanding

Not least amazing is the fact that we can discern Jesus's own understanding of his role, and can do so quite clearly behind what the first Christians subsequently thought of him. Of course, the Gospels portray Jesus as he was seen in the light of all that happened in the climax of his ministry and thereafter. But we have already seen how much of what the first believers said regarding Jesus's mission can be realistically explained only in terms of the impact Jesus made on his disciples during his mission. And so it is when we ask what we can know with confidence about Jesus's own self-awareness. The evidence can be listed quite concisely.

Jesus's Baptismal Commission

All the evangelists agree that Jesus began his mission following his baptism by John the Baptist (Mark 1:9–11 parr.). The fact that Jesus was baptized by John, implying that John was in effect senior to Jesus, was something of an embarrassment for the first Christians. Matthew indicates this by adding that John tried to prevent Jesus, saying to Jesus, "I need to be baptized by you, and do you come to me?" He only consents to baptize Jesus when Jesus replies, "Let it be so now; for it is proper for us in this way to fulfill all righteousness" (Matt 3:14–15). The point is that it was too fixed in the first followers' memory of Jesus that his mission began after his baptism by John, so that the event could hardly be ignored.

Fundamental to the earliest memory of that event was the understanding that it was then that Jesus received the affirmation of God's favor and an anointing with God's Spirit for the mission that he thereafter lived out. Whether it was a private commission, as Mark 1:10–11 implies, or something more public (Matt 3:16–17

// Luke 3:21–22), is less important than the agreed testimony of all the evangelists that Jesus's mission began from a commissioning that he received from God, his Father, when he was baptized by John.

"I Came" or "I Was Sent"

Jesus's sense of being heavenly commissioned (at his baptism by John) is attested by the number of times when he expresses that conviction. So, for example: "I have come to call not the righteous but sinners" (Mark 2:17 parr.); "I came to bring fire to the earth";[30] "the Son of Man came . . . to serve" (Mark 10:45 par.).[31] Or again: "whoever welcomes me welcomes . . . the one who sent me" (Mark 9:37 // Luke 9:48); "whoever welcomes me welcomes the one who sent me" (Matt 10:40 // John 13:20); "whoever rejects me rejects the one who sent me" (Luke 10:16). Of some interest is the fact that John elaborates the "sent" tradition,[32] indicating one of the principal roots of his more elaborate Christology. But it is clear enough that this elaboration is well rooted in the earliest memories of one who at least occasionally expressed his sense of heavenly commission in these terms. As a feature distinctive of the Gospels within the New Testament, its origin can hardly be attributed to the later believers.

Messiah/Christ

That Jesus was the long-expected Messiah is the direct implication of the information just noted. The claim is fundamental to the structure of the first three Gospels, following the lead of Mark. Although Jesus was initially hailed by demoniacs as Messiah,[33]

30. Luke 12:49, 51–53; cf. Matt 10:34–36.
31. See also Mark 1:38 // Luke 4:43 ("I was sent"); Matt 11:18–19 // Luke 7:33–34; Matt 5:17; Luke 19:10.
32. John 3:17, 34; 5:36, 38; 6:29, 57; 7:29; 8:42; 11:42; 17:3, 8, 21, 23, 25; 20:21.
33. Mark 1:24; 3:11.

Mark's account centers on Peter's confession (Mark 8:29) and climaxes in Jesus's condemnation by Pilate as "king of the Jews" (Mark 15:9–26). Because such a claim was liable to be misunderstood (in terms of political leadership), Mark shows Jesus keeping the claim quiet (Mark 1:25; 3:12) until (as already noted) he could explain that messiahship meant suffering and death, but also resurrection.[34] John's retelling of the story of Jesus's mission, in contrast, shows no such inhibitions.[35] There is no reason to doubt either that the question whether Jesus was the long-expected Messiah was raised by and during Jesus's mission, or that Jesus understood his mission in these terms, or that he was crucified as a pretentious Messiah. What is particularly interesting is that in the subsequent early Christian usage, "Christ" had already become a proper name—"Jesus Christ"—even leaving behind the affirmation "Jesus, the Christ." This suggests that the claim that Jesus was (the) Messiah was already deeply rooted at the beginnings of Christianity and entirely reflective of the messianic claim that Jesus's own mission embodied.

Abba

The Jesus tradition is quite clear that Jesus addressed God as "Father" in his prayers. All five strata of the Gospel material are unanimous on this point.[36] There are also good grounds for the further conclusion that Jesus used the Aramaic address, "Abba." The use of this term is explicitly attested in the Jesus tradition only in Mark 14:36. But since Matthew and Luke both read the Greek vocative *pater* at this point (Matt 26:39 // Luke 22:42), the probability is that underlying the vocative *pater* in the other prayers of Jesus (including the Lord's Prayer [Luke 11:2]) was the Aramaic *abba*.

34. Mark 8:31; 9:31; 10:33–34.
35. John 1:41; 4:25–26, 29.
36. Q (the source shared by Matthew and Luke)—Matt 11:25–26 // Luke 10:21; Mark 14:36 parr.; Matt 26:42; Luke 23:34, 46; John 11:41; 12:27–28; 17:1, 5, 11, 21, 24–25.

What is remarkable is that, according to Paul, the early Christians also used this intimate form of address in their prayers.[37] They attributed it to the Holy Spirit and saw it as attesting that they too were children, a status shared with Christ. The fact that the gentile (Greek-speaking) believers to whom Paul was writing regularly used this Aramaic prayer form attests how well established this form of prayer had become in the early churches. And the fact that it was seen as attesting a sonship shared with Christ is itself confirmation that the prayer language was knowingly echoing Jesus's own usage. In other words, the obvious conclusion is that the Abba prayer was so cherished among the first believers precisely because it was remembered as being Jesus's own prayer form. It was precisely because "Abba" was Jesus's own way of praying that their use of it served as assurance that they shared in his sonship.

Son of God

It is evident that Jesus was remembered as God's son by his disciples more or less from the beginning. They clearly saw his baptism in the Jordan as the occasion when he was hailed as God's "beloved son" by a heavenly voice (Mark 1:11 parr.), perhaps even as the day when he was "begotten" as God's son, as a variant text of Luke 3:22 (citing Ps 2:7) suggests. And the temptation narrative in Matthew 4 and Luke 4 focuses on precisely that status: "If you are the Son of God" (Matt 4:3, 6 // Luke 4:3, 9). Moreover, demoniacs are recalled as hailing Jesus as God's son (as in Mark 5:7 parr.).

But did Jesus see himself in these terms? The evidence is not as strong as we would like. The strongest self-testimony, Matthew 11:27 // Luke 10:22, is exceptional within the tradition shared by the first three Gospels. And one can hardly help wondering whether reference to "the Son" is a later addition to Mark 13:32 // Matthew 24:36. More plausible is the evidence of the parable of the wicked husbandmen (Mark 12:1–9 parr.), since, as we have

37. Rom 8:15–17; Gal 4:6–7.

seen, parables were a form of teaching unique to Jesus. The fact that the vineyard owner's son is killed could be a reflection of what subsequently happened to Jesus, though the absence of a clear reference to Jesus's resurrection in the parable itself suggests that its original telling expressed Jesus's own anticipation of the likely outcome of his ministry. But it does appear that the key point in the trial of Jesus was the accusation that he had claimed to be "the Christ, the son of the Blessed" (Mark 14:61). Intriguing is the fact that Matthew and Luke depict Jesus as not giving a straightforward positive answer to the accusation (Matt 26:64 // Luke 22:67–70), but nevertheless it was the charge of blasphemy that was the ground of Jesus being condemned to death. All this, along with the "Abba" evidence reviewed above, indicates that it is certainly more than plausible to deduce that the earliest Christian belief that Jesus was uniquely God's son was rooted in the earliest memories of his mission and death.

The Son of Man

The phrase "the Son of Man" occurs eighty-six times in the NT. Sixty-nine occur in the first three Gospels, and thirteen occur in John. Of the remaining four instances, three are quotations from or allusions to OT passages[38] and show no awareness of the Gospel usage. Only one titular usage ("the Son of Man") appears outside the Gospels—in Stephen's vision in Acts 7:56. Even more striking is the fact that in all four Gospels the phrase appears *only* on the lips of Jesus. He is never addressed or confessed as "Son of Man," neither in the Gospel narratives nor subsequently in the churches' worship. This is in marked contrast with other titles for Jesus. Some examples:

Mark 2:10 parr.	"That you may know that the Son of Man has authority on earth to forgive sins."

38. Heb 2:6 = Ps 8:4; Rev 1:13 and 14:14 alluding to Dan 7:13.

Mark 2:28 parr.	"The Son of Man is lord even of the sabbath."
Matt 8:20 // Luke 9:58	"Foxes have holes, and birds of the air have nests; but the Son of Man has nowhere to lay his head."
Matt 11:18–19 // Luke 7:33–34	"John came neither eating nor drinking, and they say, 'He has a demon'; the Son of Man came eating and drinking, and they say, 'Look, a glutton and a drunkard.'"

The conclusion is obvious: this particular speech usage was remembered as distinctive of Jesus precisely because that is what it was. Moreover, the several occasions on which one evangelist has "the Son of Man" while another has "I" make it clear that Jesus's first disciples recognized the phrase as a self-reference,[39] and one that was so distinctive of Jesus's own speech that it did not function as a title for Jesus in the earliest Christology of the churches. That Jesus may also have been influenced by the great vision of Daniel 7:13 hardly affects the issue,[40] though it is interesting that subsequent Christology did not make more of it. Again, the most obvious deduction is that Jesus himself was more influenced by Daniel 7:13 in the way he envisaged his ministry working out than were his immediate and subsequent disciples.

Jesus's Self-Expectation

The testimony of the Gospels is clear: Jesus fully expected death at the hands of the civil authorities (the Romans), but he also expected to be vindicated. Mark provides early hints: the warning

---

39. Luke 6:22 // Matt 5:11; Luke 12:8 // Matt 10:32; Matt 16:13 // Mark 8:27; Mark 10:45 // Luke 12:27.
40. Mark 13:26 parr.; 14:62 parr.; cf. 8:38 parr.

that he would be taken away from his disciples (Mark 2:20) and the surprisingly early indication that the Pharisees were out to get him (Mark 3:6). But the main weight of Jesus's expectation is carried by the three passion predictions that follow Peter's confession that Jesus was the Messiah (Mark 8:29).

> Then he began to teach them that the Son of Man must undergo great suffering, and be rejected by the elders, the chief priests, and the scribes, and be killed, and after three days rise again. (Mark 8:31)

> He was teaching his disciples, saying to them, "The Son of Man is to be betrayed into human hands, and they will kill him, and three days after being killed, he will rise again." (Mark 9:31)

> He took the twelve aside agian and began to tell them what was to happen to him, saying, "See, we are going up to Jerusalem, and the Son of Man will be handed over to the chief priests and the scribes, and they will condemn him to death; then they will hand him over to the Gentiles; they will mock him, and spit upon him, and flog him, and kill him; and after three days he will rise again." (Mark 10:32–34)

The fact that, despite such forewarnings, Jesus's disciples seem to have been totally unprepared for Jesus's betrayal and arrest (Mark 14:50) hardly diminishes the likelihood that Jesus himself had at least clear forebodings, even if what actually happened to Jesus understandably colored their memory of such predictions or forewarnings (as is likely in the case of Mark 10:34). For, as we have seen, there is little reason to doubt that Jesus himself was clear on the probability that his journey to Jerusalem would end with his rejection and death. So, here too we can detect clear echoes of Jesus's own self-understanding and conception of his mission.

*   *   *

There has been a tradition of scholarly skepticism stretching back two generations that very little can be said of Jesus's own self-understanding since most or almost all of the significance attributed to Jesus by the first Christians was read back by them into the memories of his prepassion mission. However, we have seen how much of Jesus's message can be attributed confidently to Jesus himself. There is in fact no good reason to deny that what has been reviewed above was rooted in good and authentic memory that Jesus's first disciples largely shared—not only the emphases and priorities that they learned from him but also the distinctive features of his ministry that they did not seek to imitate in their own ministries, and particularly what were remembered as statements and claims that revealed Jesus's own understanding of his mission and of his role. At the very least, then, we can say that the roots of the subsequent beliefs about Jesus were well established in what he was (and is) remembered as having said and how he acted. Jesus according to Jesus is firmly at the root of Jesus according to the evangelists.

CHAPTER TWO

Jesus according to

Mark, Matthew, and Luke

In a day when we are so inundated with printed material, it is hard for us to envisage centuries past when there was no printed material. We are so accustomed to daily newspapers, often with many pages. We visit bookshops with shelf upon shelf filled with new and recently published books. We can consult libraries, sometimes room after room and floor upon floor of volume after volume. Can we really envisage what it must have been like in societies when only a fairly small minority could read for themselves? When there was so little need to read, when there were so few books and parchments available to the ordinary person, when it was enough to be able to make sense of the public notices posted on public buildings? Of course, the Jewish Scripture (the Old Testament) was written, and Jewish boys may well have been trained to read the Torah. The account of Jesus reading from the Isaiah scroll in the Nazareth synagogue gives us some idea of first-century Jewish education. But it is a real question as to how many of Jesus's closest disciples could read or read well.

This is the situation we must try to envisage for the beginning of the Jesus tradition. For about thirty to forty years the memory of what Jesus had said and done would have been in *oral* form. Some scholars in the early twentieth century thought that the early memories would be of only single units—particular memories of something Jesus had said or done. But there is no reason to doubt that memories would include sequences of teaching or of events. And when stories of Jesus were told or teachings of Jesus passed on, of course they would often be in ordered form. So it is no surprise that when the Jesus tradition began to be written down we find collections of stories and sequences of integrated material.

The Gospel of Mark was to a large extent structured to include such sequences. Mark 2:1–3:6 looks like such a sequence, culminating in what would otherwise be the surprisingly early climax in the decision by Pharisees and Herodians to seek to bring Jesus down. In formulating Mark 4:1–34, it looks as though Mark was able to draw on a sequence of parables, not least to illustrate the theory of parables that he puts forward (Mark 4:11–12). Again, in framing Mark 4:35–6:52, it looks as though the author was able to draw on memories of a sequence of miracles that Jesus was remembered as having performed round the lake of Galilee. And there is general agreement among New Testament scholars that the memories of Jesus's last week climaxing in his crucifixion must have already been well established and ordered before Mark wrote his passion narrative (Mark 12:1–15:47).

Anyone who looks at a synopsis—that is, a volume in which the three Gospels (Matthew, Mark, and Luke) have been set out in parallel columns[1]—cannot help but be surprised at how close the three Gospels are to each other. I often use the phrase "the same, yet different" to bring out the striking fact that the traditions being retold in written form in these Gospels are the same, even when grouped somewhat differently, edited to some extent and addressed (presumably) to the different situations and concerns of the three authors and the communities for which they wrote. Most scholars who have specialized in the subject agree that Mark was most probably the earliest Gospel to be written, probably in the late 60s or early 70s, and that Mark was used by Matthew and Luke one or two decades later. Indeed, so much of Mark was reused by Matthew in particular that it is something of a surprise that Mark was retained as a separate Gospel. The reason

---

1. "Synopsis," literally "seen together."

may simply be the strong tradition that Mark had acted as Peter's secretary and that it was Peter's memories and preaching that he had written down.

Here we should include the strong opinion among most scholars that as well as Mark, the two others of the threesome, Matthew and Luke, had been able to draw on another source. This is indicated by the large amount of non-Markan material in Matthew and Luke that is more or less the same. The non-Markan material common to Matthew and Luke has become known as Q, an unimaginative abbreviation for the German *Quelle* (source). One of the great and thus far unresolved debates in Gospel scholarship is how much of Q was already written. Were Matthew and Luke able to draw on a single written collection of Jesus's teaching for their non-Markan material? Dependence on a written source is clear, in a passage like Matthew 3:7–10, 12 // Luke 3:7–9, 17. But elsewhere the agreement between Matthew and Luke can be as little as 8 percent. So it is quite possible that in a fair number of cases Matthew and Luke were drawing on differing oral accounts of the same events and teaching. Here again, then, the degree of variation in the synoptic material shows how varied was the Jesus tradition—the same, yet different. It is quite important to note that whatever form the Q document took, it was not retained as such. It recounted the teaching of Jesus, but Jesus was not to be remembered simply as a great teacher. So Q was valued and its material retained only as integrated into the written Gospel tradition.

Mark

It was Mark who gave us the *written* Gospel. Indeed, it was Mark to whom we should attribute the idea of a "gospel" as an account of Jesus's ministry, death, and resurrection. Prior to Mark, Paul had taken a term that was most used in the plural in reference to the emperor's activities.[2] Paul had focused attention on the singular—the good news—and used it to sum up the good news of

2. See further, ch. 5 below.

Jesus's death and resurrection. In effect he was saying to the wider Roman public that *the* good news, *the* gospel, is not about Caesar but about Jesus.

But it is Mark who introduces the term "gospel" (*euangelion*) into the Jesus tradition itself. He uses the term seven times, whereas the longer Matthew uses it only four times, and Luke and John not at all. What is notable is that Mark's use seems to be consistently his own—most notably in the very opening of his account:

Mark 1:1   "The beginning of the gospel of Jesus Christ."

Mark 1:14–15   "Jesus came to Galilee, proclaiming the gospel of God . . . ; 'repent, and believe in the gospel.'"[3]

In Mark's opening words, in fact, we see the transition taking place from the gospel as the good news of Jesus's death and resurrection to the now more familiar sense of the gospel as the good news of Jesus's whole mission, climaxing in his death and resurrection. It was Mark to whom we owe that understanding and use of the word "gospel."

It is worth noting some key features of the Gospel of Mark, three in particular.

Passion Narratives with an Introduction

In a famous note Martin Kähler described the Gospels as "passion narratives with extended introductions."[4] This is particularly

---

3. The underlining indicates that the underlined wording is unique to Mark, who also did not hesitate to add the word elsewhere to elaborate the Jesus tradition and to bring out the force of the gospel now set out in his Gospel: Mark 8:35—"Those who lose their life for my sake, and for the sake of the gospel, will save it"; Mark 10:29—"He who has left home . . . for my sake and for the sake of the gospel will receive a hundredfold."

4. Martin Kähler, *The So-Called Historical Jesus and the Historic Biblical Christ* (Philadelphia: Fortress, 1964), 80n11.

true of Mark's Gospel and helps explain how the transition in the meaning of the term "gospel" took place.

The appropriateness of Kähler's description is shown by various features in the Gospel of Mark:

- The lengthy climax, the last week of Jesus's ministry, is given such prominence (Mark 11:1–16:8).
- The three passion predictions dominate the three chapters beginning the second half of the Gospel—Mark 8:31, 9:31, and 10:33–34. For example, Mark 9:31: "The Son of Man is to be betrayed into human hands, and they will kill him, and three days after being killed, he will rise again."
- Most striking are the early anticipations of the Gospel's climax: "The days will come when the bridegroom is taken away" (Mark 2:20); "The Pharisees . . . conspired . . . against him, how to destroy him" (Mark 3:6); "The cup that I drink [and] . . . the baptism with which I am baptized" (Mark 10:39); and the parable of the vineyard leased to tenants (Mark 12:1–12).

Kähler's description is well justified.

The Messianic Secret

At the beginning of the twentieth century, William Wrede drew attention to a fascinating feature of Mark's Gospel that he designated "the messianic secret."[5] The particular features of the Gospel to which Wrede drew attention and which provided the justification for his use of the phrase were numerous and quite striking. Considered individually, they might not amount to much. But taken together, they build into a strong case.

5. William Wrede, *Das Messiasgeheimnis in den Evangelien: Zugleich ein Beitrag zum Verständnis des Markusevangeliums* (Göttingen: Vandenhoeck & Ruprecht, 1901). English translation: William Wrede, *The Messianic Secret*, trans. J. C. G. Greig (Cambridge: James Clarke, 1971).

An immediately striking feature is Jesus's *commands to silence*—the implication being that Jesus wanted his activity, or rather the significance of that activity, not to be known more widely, since presumably it would be heard of by the authorities, who might intervene sooner than he wanted.

Mark 1:34	"[Jesus] would not permit the demons to speak, because they knew him."
Mark 1:44	Jesus commanded the cleansed leper: "See that you say nothing to anyone."
Mark 3:12	"He [Jesus] sternly ordered [the unclean spirits] not to make him known."
Mark 5:43	"He [Jesus] strictly ordered" those who had come to mourn the death of Jairus's daughter that "no one should know" of her restoration to full active life.
Mark 8:30	Following Peter's confession of Jesus to be the Messiah, "He [Jesus] strictly ordered [the disciples] not to tell anyone about him."
Mark 9:9	Similarly, following their witness of his transfigured presence on a mountain, together with Moses and Elijah, "He [Jesus] ordered them to tell no one about what they had seen."

Probably in the same category we should put Jesus's repeated *desire to remain hidden*, away from the crowds—evident in several passages. Note the following:

Mark 1:35	Very early in the morning Jesus "went out to a deserted place, and there he prayed."

Mark 6:45–46   Jesus "made his disciples get into the boat and go on ahead to the other side." After dismissing the crowd, "he went up on the mountain to pray."[6]

Equally striking, for the same reason, is the number of occasions when Jesus is recalled as *healing in private*:

Mark 5:37, 40   In the healing of Jairus's daughter, "He [Jesus] allowed no one to follow him except Peter, James, and John."

Mark 7:33   "He took [the deaf man] aside in private, away from the crowd," and healed him.

Mark 8:23   "He took the blind man by the hand and led him out of the village" and healed him.

The other striking feature of the Gospel of Mark noted by Wrede in this connection is the number of occasions when Mark emphasizes that Jesus gave *private instruction* to his disciples.

Mark 4:34   "He did not speak to [the crowds] except in parables, but he explained everything in private to his disciples."

Mark 7:17   "When he had left the crowd and entered the house, his disciples asked about the parable."

Mark 9:28   Following the healing of the epileptic boy, Jesus "entered the house," where "his disciples asked him privately."

Mark 13:3   On the Mount of Olives, "Peter, James, John, and Andrew asked him privately."[7]

6. See also Mark 1:45 and 3:7, 9.
7. Note also Mark 6:31–32 and 9:2.

So Wrede's highlighting of what seems to be a consistent emphasis in Mark's Gospel is well justified.

Mark's Ending

One of the most striking features of Mark's Gospel is its ending. On the Sunday following Jesus's crucifixion, the story of the empty tomb is left hanging unresolved. All we are left with is the promise of the mysterious "young man" discovered sitting in the empty tomb (an angel or Mark himself?) to cheer the women who made the disturbing discovery. The reassurance was that Jesus had been raised (from the dead) and would go ahead of them to Galilee where they would see him (Mark 16:7).

And that is about it! The Gospel then ends rather abruptly. Apparently content with the promise just given, the women "went out and fled from the tomb, for terror and amazement had seized them; and they said nothing to anyone, for they were afraid" (Mark 16:8).

Apparently that is how Mark intended to end his Gospel—a devastating discovery (the empty tomb); a rather puzzling promise from a strange, unidentified "young man"; and the women's departure from the tomb, not full of joy but fearful and full of terror! No wonder Mark's ending was regarded by some (or many!) as inadequate and attempts were made to provide a more satisfactory, more positive ending. Both a shorter and a longer alternative ending were added later and appear in most translations. But they do not resolve the issue of why Mark himself ended his Gospel in the way he did. Of course, Mark would have known that the house groups and congregations where his Gospel was read would themselves know the fuller story. And perhaps Mark wrote in effect to encourage such gatherings to carry on the story with accounts of resurrection appearances and of their own experiences of the risen Christ. But the way he actually did end his Gospel remains something of a puzzle.

Matthew

Matthew absorbed almost all of Mark in his Gospel, but by elaborating it with Q material and rearranging the order and grouping of the tradition, he produced a quite different way of telling the good news (gospel) of Jesus.

Structure

The most obvious distinctive features are immediately apparent. Matthew starts his Gospel by pushing back the beginning of his account of Jesus from Jesus's baptism to his birth (Matt 1–2). And he also provides a better conclusion (Matt 28:1–20). Again, while Mark emphasized Jesus's role as teacher, Matthew has provided more teaching. Nor should it be missed that Matthew has put Jesus's teaching into five "sermons" at Matthew 5:3–7:27, 10:5–42, 13:3–52, 18:1–35, and 24:2–25:46. What signals the "sermons" is the way Matthew concludes them:

Matt 7:28   "Now when Jesus had finished saying these things."

Matt 11:1   "When Jesus had finished instructing his twelve disciples."

Matt 13:53   "When Jesus had finished these parables."

Matt 19:1   "When Jesus had finished saying these things."

Matt 26:1   "When Jesus had finished saying all these things."

Christology

More striking is the way Matthew develops the Christology of his Gospel, well beyond that of Mark. For Matthew, Jesus not only brings wisdom from God, but Jesus himself embodies the divine presence. This becomes clear in a number of passages unique to Matthew. Thus most clearly in his opening chapter: "'The virgin shall conceive and bear a son, and they shall name him Emmanuel,' which means, 'God is with us'" (Matt 1:23). Bolder still is the way in which Matthew identifies Jesus with divine Wisdom— Wisdom being the figure that or who in the book of Proverbs and the wisdom literature of Israel is a way of speaking of the divine presence. Thus at the beginning of chapter 11, in a passage again distinctive of his Gospel, Matthew notes that "John, who was in prison, heard about the *deeds* of the Messiah" (Matt 11:2 NIV) and concludes the following story by quoting Jesus referring to the distinctiveness of his ministry with the claim that "[W]isdom is vindicated by her *deeds*" (Matt 11:19). Equally striking is the allusion that Matthew has Jesus uniquely making to a famous passage in Israel's wisdom literature:

Sir 51:25–26   "Acquire wisdom for yourselves. . . . Put your neck under her yoke."

Matt 11:29   "Take my yoke upon you, and learn from me."

The yoke of Wisdom is now Jesus's yoke! Equally striking is the fact that whereas Luke 11:49 records Jesus as saying, "the Wisdom of God said, 'I will send them prophets and apostles, some of whom they will kill and persecute,'" Matthew 23:34 attributes Wisdom's words to Jesus himself. Jesus says, "I send you prophets . . . some of whom you will kill."

The Fulfillment of Jewish Expectation

Another notable feature of Matthew's Christology is the unique extent to which he goes in presenting the coming and ministry of Jesus as the fulfillment of Jewish expectation. All the scriptural quotations are introduced with a clear indication of a prophecy fulfilled—typically, "All this took place to fulfill what had been spoken by the Lord through the prophet."

Matt 1:23	"The virgin shall conceive and bear a son" (Isa 7:14).
Matt 2:15	"Out of Egypt I have called my son" (Hos 11:1).
Matt 2:23	"He will be called a Nazorean" (source is unknown).
Matt 4:14–16	"The people who sat in darkness have seen a great light" (Isa 8:23–9:1).
Matt 8:17	"He took our infirmities and bore our diseases" (Isa 53:4).
Matt 12:18–21	"Here is my servant, whom I have chosen, my beloved, with whom my soul is well pleased. I will put my Spirit upon him" (Isa 42:1–4).

It can even be argued that Matthew sought to present Jesus as *a new Moses*. This presumably is the implication of the identification of Jesus with Israel's exodus from Egypt in the passage just quoted: "Out of Egypt I have called my son" (Matt 2:15). The fact already noted that Matthew has grouped the teaching of Jesus into five blocks suggests that Matthew wanted his presentation of Jesus's teaching to be seen as echoing or fulfilling the five books of Moses. And we can hardly fail to note the passage, unique to Matthew, in which Jesus strongly affirms the law.

> Do not think that I have come to abolish the law or the prophets; I have come not to abolish but to fulfill. For truly I tell you, until heaven and earth pass away, not one letter, not one stroke of a letter, will pass from the law until all is accomplished. . . . For I tell you, unless your righteousness exceeds that of the scribes and Pharisees, you will never enter the kingdom of heaven. (Matt 5:17–20)

Would Paul have recognized that teaching? Would he have accepted that teaching? How often I wish I could have listened in on some of the earliest Christian debates—not least in this case and in reference to the law and its continuing validity for Jesus's followers.

Focus on Israel

Another striking feature of Matthew is that he saw the focus of Jesus's ministry to be Israel itself. Particularly remarkable are the passages unique to Matthew, indicated by underlining:

Matt 1:21 "He will save his people from their sins."

Matt 2:6 "From you [Bethlehem] shall come a ruler who is to shepherd my people Israel."

Matt 10:5–6 "Go nowhere among the Gentiles . . . but go rather to the lost sheep of the house of Israel."

Matt 15:24 "I was sent only to the lost sheep of the house of Israel."

Matt 19:28 Jesus and his disciples will judge "the twelve tribes of Israel" (cf. Luke 22:30).

At the same time, we should note Matthew's own openness to and affirmation that the mission of Jesus's disciples included the gentiles.

Matt 1:3–6 It should not escape notice that the genealogy of Jesus at the opening of Matthew's Gospel includes three named women—Tamar, Rahab, and Ruth—all of them gentiles.

Matt 3:9 John the Baptist is recalled as preaching, "Do not presume to say to yourselves, 'We have Abraham as our ancestor.'"

Matt 8:11–12	Jesus reminds his audience that "many will come from east and west and will eat with Abraham and Isaac and Jacob in the kingdom of heaven, while the heirs of the kingdom will be thrown into the outer darkness."
Matt 21:43	Matthew ends the parable of the wicked tenants by warning that "the kingdom of God will be taken away from you and given" to others.
Matt 22:8–9	The parable of the marriage feast is equally foreboding, with its warning that those who had rejected the summons to the wedding feast would be replaced by others.

Matthew confirms that the gospel is for all nations (Matt 24:14, taking up Mark 13:10) and ends his Gospel with Jesus's commission that his disciples are to "Go . . . and make disciples of all nations" (Matt 28:19). Evidently Matthew did not want it to be forgotten that Jesus saw his own mission as primarily for his own people. But he was equally concerned to note that Jesus forewarned against too much being made of that fact, since the death and resurrection of Jesus opened the gospel to "all nations."

Reaffirmation of the Law

We have already noted the strong reaffirmation of the law by Matthew's Jesus (Matt 5:17–20). Particularly striking is his record of warnings made by Jesus against *anomia*, "lawlessness." These warnings occur several times in Matthew[8] and, notably, are unique to Matthew. He certainly recalls Jesus as refining the law, but he would hardly have accepted that Jesus abrogated the law of Moses.

8. Matt 7:23; 13:41; 23:28; 24:12.

In fact, one of the principal features of the Gospel of Matthew is his record of Jesus reaffirming and redefining the law in contest with various Pharisees. So the Sermon on the Mount sharpens the laws on murder (Matt 5:21–22) and adultery (Matt 5:27–28). He recalls Jesus as redefining and summarizing "the law and the prophets" with the Golden Rule: "In everything do to others as you would have them do to you" (Matt 7:12). He records Jesus as on two occasions summarizing the law in the words of Hosea 6:6: "I desire mercy, not sacrifice" (Matt 9:13; 12:7). All these are unparalleled and distinctive of Matthew. Furthermore, Matthew recalls Jesus as giving higher priority in terms of purity to what comes out of the mouth than to what goes into the mouth (Matt 15:17–20). Mark presses home the point by inferring that "Thus Jesus declared all foods clean," but Matthew maintains that Jesus is only relativizing the laws of clean and unclean. Again Matthew does not hesitate to recall Jesus as summing up "all the law and the prophets" in the twofold command: first, to love God with all your being, and second, to love your neighbor as yourself (Matt 22:37–40). Distinctive of Matthew is his recollection of Jesus's condemnation of scribes and Pharisees for disregarding the law and for putting more weight on outward appearance (Matt 23:2–3). His record of Jesus condemning them as "serpents" and a "brood of vipers" (Matt 23:33) presumably reflects the tension that must have built up between Jesus's Jewish followers and the Jewish teachers. Though we should not forget Matthew 24:20, where Jesus urges his disciples to pray in the case of catastrophe, "that your flight may not be in winter or on a sabbath." It is hard to escape the sense that some at least of such passages reflect the tribulations that Jesus's disciples faced later in the first century.

Luke

Luke brings home even more clearly than Matthew that the same story (of Jesus) can be told differently. A vivid illustration is the fact that it is only Luke who records some of Jesus's most enduring parables: for example, the good Samaritan (Luke 10:25–37), the prodigal son (Luke 15:11–32), the rich man and Lazarus (Luke 16:19–31), and the Pharisee and the tax collector (Luke 18:9–14). Other features make Luke stand out among the Gospels.

Anointed by the Spirit

Luke emphasizes *the Spirit*—the underlining indicating material unique to Luke:

Luke 1:15	Even before his birth: "He [the Baptist] will be filled with the Holy Spirit."
Luke 1:35	"The Holy Spirit will come upon you [Mary] . . . ; therefore the child to be born will be holy; he will be called Son of God."
Luke 1:67	"Zechariah [the Baptist's father] was filled with the Holy Spirit and spoke this prophecy: . . ."
Luke 2:25–27	"The Holy Spirit rested on [Simeon]. It had been revealed to him by the Holy Spirit." He had been "guided by the Spirit."
Luke 4:1, 14	"Jesus, full of the Holy Spirit, returned from the Jordan and was led by the Spirit [to be tempted]."
Luke 4:18	"The Spirit of the Lord is upon me, because he has anointed me to bring good news to the poor."
Luke 10:21	"Jesus rejoiced in the Holy Spirit and said . . ." (cf. Matt 11:27).[9]

9. See also Luke 1:17; 11:13.

In this, of course, Luke no doubt had in mind his intention to write a second volume, narrating the beginning of the Jesus or Christian movement following Jesus's death and resurrection. In that volume, as we shall see, the Holy Spirit is the most prominent actor, starting with Pentecost, the inspiring power that drove the early mission of Jesus's disciples forward with great success. It is not at all surprising, therefore, that Luke took the opportunity, in his own retelling of the gospel story given by Mark, to bring out just how much Jesus's own ministry was at the instigation of God's Spirit and was endowed with the power of that same Spirit. Notably, Luke did not add many Spirit references to the Markan account itself, but he certainly took pains to affirm that the Baptist's and Jesus's births were hailed by the Spirit and that Jesus's anointing by the Spirit was a strong feature of the beginnings of Jesus's ministry.

Mission to Sinners

Equally notable and distinctive is Luke's emphasis that Jesus's mission was to *sinners*— the underlining again indicating material only in Luke:

Luke 5:8	Simon Peter says: "Go away from me, Lord, for I am a sinful man!"
Luke 5:30, 32	In response to criticism that he ate and drank with sinners, Jesus replies: "I have come to call . . . sinners to repentance."
Luke 7:34	"The Son of Man has come eating and drinking, and you say, 'Look, . . . a friend of tax collectors and sinners!'"
Luke 7:37–38	Jesus is anointed by a woman "who was a sinner."
Luke 15:2	Jesus is criticized by Pharisees and scribes: "This fellow welcomes sinners and eats with them."

Luke 15:7, cf. 10   "There will be more joy in heaven over one sinner who repents than over ninety-nine righteous persons."

Luke 18:13   In the parable of the Pharisee and the tax collector, the latter prays, "God, be merciful to me, a sinner!"

Luke 19:7   When Jesus invites himself to Zacchaeus's house, the crowd murmurs: "He has gone to be the guest of one who is a sinner."

Of interest here is the fact that Luke does not use the word "sinner" in his second volume (Acts). So it can hardly be said that he focused on this aspect of Jesus's mission because it was such a prominent feature of the earliest mission of the apostles. Equally striking is the fact that in the Gospel of Luke the term "sinner" appears much more often than in the other canonical Gospels.[10] So, clearly, Luke saw this as a very important aspect of Jesus's ministry and drew on the Jesus tradition to bring out the importance of this aspect. Indeed, it appears from Luke's account that Jesus made a point of associating with the religiously (and socially) unacceptable and indeed sought them out. This practice shows as clearly as anything Jesus said that he did not see his mission or his responsibility to others to be determined by the social and religious conventions of the day—a thought that the religious establishments that sprang from his mission ought never to forget.

Good News for Gentiles

Another emphasis of Luke is that the good news of Jesus is also for gentiles. Most notable are again distinctive features of Luke's recollection and use of the Jesus tradition.

10. "Sinner"—eighteen times in Luke, six in Mark, five in Matthew, and four in John.

Luke 2:29–32	Simeon's prophecy regarding the infant Jesus: "... a light for revelation to the Gentiles ..."
Luke 3:6	Luke makes a point of extending the Baptist's quotation of Isa 40:3–5 right to the end: "... and all flesh shall see the salvation of God."
Luke 4:26–27	Luke extends the account of Jesus's sermon in Nazareth to remind the hearers that Elijah was sent only to the widow at Zarephath, and Elisha healed only Naaman the Syrian.
Luke 10:25–37	The parable of the good Samaritan.
Luke 17:11–19	The healing of ten lepers, of whom only the Samaritan returns to give Jesus thanks.

As with his emphasis on the Spirit, Luke's Gospel prepares for the greater emphasis of his second volume, particularly the commission of Saul/Paul, which Luke emphasizes three times.[11] It was no doubt fundamental for Luke that the great expansion of the Jesus movement to the gentiles, which he was to record and of which he himself had been part, was entirely consistent with Jesus's own mission. The comparison of Matthew and Luke raises interesting speculations as to what the authors would have said to each other with regard to the other's version of the gospel.

Frequent Prayer

One of the most interesting features of Luke's Gospel is the prominence he gives to the fact that Jesus *prayed* frequently. He alone notes that the descent of the Spirit on Jesus came when Jesus "had been baptized and was praying" (Luke 3:21). Luke alone

---

11. Acts 9:15; 22:15; 26:17–18.

notes that after healing a leper Jesus "withdrew to the wilderness and prayed" (Luke 5:16 RSV). He alone records that before Jesus chose the Twelve he "went out to the mountain to pray; and he spent the night in prayer to God" (Luke 6:12). Again it is Luke alone who records that the conversation leading to the confession of Peter came "when Jesus was praying alone" and "the disciples [were] near him" (Luke 9:18). It is only Luke who records that the transfiguration happened when Jesus "went up on the mountain to pray"; and that it was "while he was praying" that Jesus was transfigured (Luke 9:28–29). Only Luke introduces the Lord's Prayer by noting that it was as Jesus "was praying in a certain place" that one of his disciples asked to be taught "to pray, as John taught his disciples" (Luke 11:1). We might mention also that only Luke tells the parables of the unjust judge and of the Pharisee and the tax collector (Luke 18:2–14), both about effective prayer, and that he introduces the parables by noting that Jesus told them "about their need to pray always and not to lose heart" (Luke 18:1). Finally, it is only Luke who records that Jesus introduced his time of prayer in Gethsemane by urging his disciples, "Pray that you may not come into the time of trial" (Luke 22:40), and that "in his anguish he prayed more earnestly" (Luke 22:44).

Of course, Luke also emphasizes that the mission of the disciples in his second volume was equally marked by prayer—including, for example, the choice of a twelfth disciple to replace Judas (Acts 1:24), the appointment of the seven to assist the apostles (Acts 6:6), the converted Saul of Tarsus (Acts 9:11), the breakthrough with the gentile Cornelius (Acts 10:9, 30; 11:5), the commissioning of Barnabas and Saul to mission (Acts 13:3), and at various points in Paul's missionary work.[12] It is clear, then, that for Luke missionary work was impossible to conceive without prayer—as documented not only by the mission of the earliest church but also by the mission of Jesus himself.

---

12. Acts 14:23; 16:25; 20:36; 21:5; 22:17; 28:8.

Jesus as Lord

An interesting if fairly minor feature is the way the evangelists refer to Jesus as "Lord." "Lord," of course, has a range of denotation, used both regularly in the sense of "sir" and in reference to God—"the Lord." In the Gospels, Jesus is quite naturally described as "the lord" or "master,"[13] or more frequently addressed as "lord" or "sir."[14] Moreover, "Lord" is the obvious connotation from the earliest days of the Christian church—"the Lord Jesus" being a common reference, for example, particularly in Paul. The implication is that the corollary to Jesus's crucifixion, that is, his resurrection and ascension, exalted Jesus to a status that transformed the polite *kyrios*, denoting social recognition of a higher authority, into *Kyrios*, with the connotation of lordship, of a heavenly lordship, where Psalm 110:1 could be taken more or less literally.[15] Luke deserves mention here because he alone notes that Jesus was first referred to as "the Lord" by one of his contemporaries, in Luke 24:34. We might even say that the first Christian message accompanied the realization that Jesus was not gone from them—when the disciples on the road to Emmaus realized that the person who had walked with them from Jerusalem was in fact the risen Jesus, and in reporting it they gave what in effect was the first Christian confession, "The Lord has risen indeed."

13. E.g., Matt 21:3; 24:42; Mark 11:3; Luke 7:13; 10:1, 39, 41; 11:39; 13:15; 17:5, 6; 18:6; 19:8, 31, 34; 22:33, 38, 61.

14. E.g., Matt 8:2, 6, 8, 21, 25; 14:28, 30; 15:22, 25, 27; 20:30, 31, 33; Luke 5:8, 12; 7:6; 9:54, 59, 61; 10:17, 40; 12:41; 13:23; 17:37; 18:41.

15. Note how often Ps 110:1 is referred to or quoted in the New Testament—more than any other verse from the Hebrew Bible in Greek translation—Matt 22:44; 26:64; Mark 12:36; 14:62; [16:19]; Luke 20:42; 22:69; Acts 2:34; Rom 8:34; 1 Cor 15:25; Eph 1:20; Heb 1:3, 13; 8:1; 10:12. See also the beginning of chapter 4.

The Perils of Wealth and Concern for the Poor

Luke is notable for the warnings against *the perils of wealth* that appear regularly in his Gospel, usually his own emphasis.[16]

Luke 1:53	Mary magnifies the Lord: "he has filled the hungry with good things, and sent the rich away empty."
Luke 6:20, 24	The beatitudes in Luke are distinctive: "Blessed are you who are poor. . . . But woe to you who are rich."
Luke 12:13–21	The parable of the rich but shortsighted landowner.
Luke 12:33	"Sell your possessions, and give alms" (cf. Matt 6:19).
Luke 16:19–31	The parable of the rich man and Lazarus.
Luke 18:18–25	The sad story of the rich young ruler, unwilling to give up his possessions (cf. Matt 19:16–24 // Mark 10:25).
Luke 19:1–10	The story of Zacchaeus, the wealthy tax collector, climaxing in his giving half of his goods to the poor and restoring anything defrauded fourfold.

Equally striking is Luke's *concern for the poor*— the underlining again indicating material unique to Luke:[17]

---

16. The word *plousios* (rich, wealthy) appears in Luke eleven times; contrast three in Matthew, two in Mark, and none in John.

17. The word "poor" appears in Luke twice as often as it does in Matthew or Mark.

Luke 1:46–55	Mary's Magnificat well sets the tone: God "<u>has filled the hungry with good things, and sent the rich away empty</u>" (Luke 1:53).
Luke 4:18	Jesus reads from Isaiah in the synagogue: "<u>The Spirit of the Lord . . . has anointed me to bring good news to the poor</u>" (Isa 61:1–2).
Luke 6:20	In some contrast to Matt 5:3 ("Blessed are the poor in spirit"), Luke records Jesus as saying, "Blessed are you . . . poor."
Luke 14:13	"<u>When you give a banquet, invite the poor.</u>"
Luke 14:15–24	The parable of the great dinner, when the original guests refuse to come and invitations are issued to "<u>the poor, the crippled, the blind, and the lame.</u>"
Luke 16:19–31	<u>The parable of the rich man and Lazarus.</u>
Luke 18:22	Again the sad story of the rich young man who failed to respond to Jesus's challenge: "There is still one thing lacking. Sell all that you own and distribute the money to the poor."
Luke 19:8	Zacchaeus's response to Jesus's intervention: "<u>Half of my possessions . . . I will give to the poor.</u>"

Again, rather strikingly, neither the word "poor" nor the word "rich" appears in Luke's second volume, the Acts of the Apostles. So, once again we have to conclude that the emphasis on the subject in Luke's Gospel must reflect the fact that this was indeed one of Jesus's own major emphases. On the other hand, we should not fail to notice the concern shown in the earliest gatherings of Jesus's disciples in Jerusalem for those who were being neglected in the daily distribution from the community of goods (Acts 6:1–6; referring back to 2:44–45). The letter of James has one of the strongest passages in the NT on the importance of showing proper care and respect for the poor (Jas 2:1–7). Nor should we forget that Paul laid great emphasis on the collection he was making among the new churches he had established for "the poor among the saints at Jerusalem" (Rom 15:26)—a consistent emphasis in Paul's ministry to try to ensure the unity of all the growing churches (Gal 2:10; 2 Cor 8–9). It is sobering to remember that it was Paul's determination to deliver that collection to Jerusalem that resulted in his arrest and ended in his death. Such concern for the poor among Jesus's disciples was of course well rooted in the Old Testament. But who can doubt that Jesus was well remembered by the first Christians as reinforcing that concern and its priority among believers?

The Role of Women

Finally, it is hardly inappropriate to notice that Luke highlights the role of women in Jesus's entry into the world and among his disciples.

Luke 1:25, 46–55	The prominence given to the mother of the Baptist (Elizabeth) and the mother of Jesus (Mary) is striking.
Luke 8:2–3	Only Luke mentions the women who were Jesus's backups.
Luke 10:38–42	Only Luke tells the story of Martha and Mary.
Luke 18:2–5	Only Luke relates the parable of the unjust judge giving way to a woman's badgering.
Luke 23:27–29	Only Luke reports Jesus's words to the women who lamented as Jesus was led to Golgotha: "Daughters of Jerusalem . . . weep for yourselves and for your children."

Here it is well to note the prominence of women among Paul's various mission teams. Indeed, as already noted, a calculation made in regard to Paul's various colleagues and associates in mission reveals that about 20 percent of such colleagues were women—an astonishing fact for its time. The list of greetings that Paul makes in Romans 16 well illustrates the point. The point needs some emphasis in view of the common impression that Paul was antipathetic to women's ministry. So it should be restated that, in a day where women's role in ministry and mission was minimal, Paul's mission teams were exceptional. And from where did Paul gain such a perspective and policy out of keeping with his times? Where else than Jesus and the example he had set?

*   *   *

Some important points emerging from what we have seen above should be underlined. First, the ministry and teaching of Jesus were not put into writing straightaway, neither during his ministry nor directly thereafter. But the thirty to forty years of written silence hardly mean that the memories of what Jesus had done and taught had been lost or forgotten. On the contrary, the evidence of the synoptic tradition is that accounts of what Jesus was remembered as having done and said circulated and were passed on in various forms and combinations.

Second, the character of what Jesus had taught and done is clear from the Jesus tradition in its varied forms. "The same, yet different" well summarizes the twin character of the synoptic tradition. In short, the Jesus tradition gives a clear impression in two directions—the impression/impact made by Jesus on his first disciples, and the different ways the memories of Jesus's ministry were conveyed to new disciples and churches.

Third, the summary term "gospel" was claimed for the Christian movement for its central message by Paul, and given its technical Christian sense by Mark. If "gospel" as a Christian term is defined by Mark, as the story of Jesus's ministry, climaxing in his death and resurrection, then later uses of the term, as in the Gospel of Thomas, are better described as a misuse of the term.

Fourth, particularly by framing his telling of the story of Jesus's ministry as the unveiling of "the messianic secret" of Jesus, Mark added a spice to what might otherwise have been a more pedestrian account. And his ending of the story, leaving the hearer in some suspense, presumably helped bring a listening audience to their own experience of the risen Jesus.

Fifth, Matthew's retelling of the Gospel of Mark shows how adaptable was the Jesus tradition—how different emphases could be brought out from the same tradition. In Matthew's case the emphases seem to have been to make his Gospel more appealing to Jewish audiences—the five blocks of Jesus's teaching mirroring the five books of Moses, the Wisdom Christology, the emphasis on Jesus as the fulfillment of Jewish expectation, the focus on Jesus's mission to Israel, and the reaffirmation of the law. It is this sense of Jesus's continuity with what had gone before in God's leading of Israel that most marks the Gospel of Matthew and makes it distinctive among the documents of the New Testament.

Sixth, if Matthew links the ministry of Jesus most firmly to God's dealings with Israel in the past, Luke points, with equal firmness, to the potential of Jesus's mission for the gentile world. This is most obvious in his emphasis on the role of the Spirit, to be continued in his second volume, as also Jesus's own openness to gentiles. Distinctive of Luke, but also of powerful significance for Luke's wider concerns evidenced in Acts, are his emphasis on Jesus's ministry among sinners, his note that Jesus gave priority to prayer during his own ministry, Jesus's concern for the poor, and the importance of the role of women in Jesus's ministry.

Jesus according to Mark, Matthew, and Luke comes across as certainly the same Jesus, but the same Jesus powerfully impacting different people and different situations. What if only one Gospel had been treasured by the earliest churches—giving the impression that there was only one acceptable way of telling the story of Jesus's ministry, that there was only one way in which his teaching could be retained and passed on correctly? Thankfully, Jesus's ministry was told diversely from the first, not least in order that the diversity of its appeal should be maintained.

CHAPTER THREE

Jesus according to

John

I t is natural to assume that the Gospel of John is just like the other three Gospels contained in the New Testament. Natural because they are telling the story of the same life—the ministry of Jesus. But when the Gospel of John is set out in parallel columns with the other three (Matthew, Mark, and Luke), it almost immediately becomes evident that John is different from the others. As already noted, with the Synoptics, Matthew, Mark, and Luke, the parallels are very close. Apart from the two opening chapters of Matthew and Luke, the degree of overlap in all three, often almost word-for-word parallels, is very striking. One of the most interesting experiences of my early days of scholarship was to underline the parallels between the three Synoptics—red indicating where Matthew and Luke seem to have copied Mark, blue for the non-Markan agreements between Matthew and Luke usually referred to as Q, and yellow for passages distinctive to each Gospel. That is why they are called Synoptics, because they can so easily be "seen together."

But with John it is different. John is telling the same story, of the same person. But he is telling it differently. For example, early on John indicates that Jesus's miracles should be regarded as "signs," indicating the significance of the miracle-worker. So the first miracle recorded, turning the water into wine (John 2:1–10), is rounded off by noting that this was "the first of his signs . . . and revealed his glory" (John 2:11). The following references to Jesus's "signs" (John 2:23; 3:2; 4:54) reinforce John's point that he was not just telling the story of mighty works performed by Jesus, but was drawing out the significance of what Jesus did and said.[1] In effect, he makes the same point by regularly attaching long discourses to his accounts of the miracles performed by Jesus. So, for example, the feeding of the five thousand leads into the great bread of life discourse (John 6); the healing of the blind man leads into Jesus's speaking about blindness and sight (John 9); and the raising of Lazarus is integrated with the discourse on eternal life (John 11).

When John is compared with the Synoptics, a striking feature is that John contains no real parables; the nearest is when Jesus is recorded as saying "I am the true vine" (15:1–6). In fact, it is the "I am" sayings that seem to function as John's equivalent to the synoptic parables.

John 6:35	"I am the bread of life."
John 8:12	"I am the light of the world."
John 8:58	"Before Abraham was, I am."
John 10:11	"I am the good shepherd."
John 11:25	"I am the resurrection and the life."
John 14:6	"I am the way, and the truth, and the life."
John 15:1	"I am the true vine."

It is a striking fact that these "I am" sayings appear only in the Fourth Gospel. It is almost impossible to believe that there

---

1. See also 6:2, 14, 26; 7:31; 9:16; 11:47; 12:18, 37; 20:30. It was for this reason that C. H. Dodd, in a famous work, *The Interpretation of the Fourth Gospel* (Cambridge: Cambridge University Press, 1960), called John 2–12 "the Book of Signs."

were such sayings in the Jesus tradition, sayings that Jesus was remembered as uttering about himself, and yet all three synoptic evangelists ignored them completely. Much the more obvious explanation is that these were sayings attributed to Jesus by John not because he was remembered as uttering them, but because they brought out the significance of Jesus and his ministry like nothing else in the Jesus tradition, confirming the significance of his ministry and miracles.

So the obvious conclusion to draw with regard to John is that, unlike the authors of the Synoptics, he was *not* trying to give a more or less straightforward account of Jesus's ministry. Rather, he sought to bring out the *significance* of Jesus's ministry and his death and resurrection. What is important, when we compare the so-called gospels that followed in the second and third centuries, is that John retained the Gospel format, established by Mark, beginning with John the Baptist and climaxing in Jesus's crucifixion and resurrection. But his Gospel is more a *reflection* on Jesus's ministry and on Jesus himself, drawing on the tradition of Jesus's miracle working, and in effect elaborating things that Jesus was remembered as saying to draw out the significance of the signs and of the revelation of God that Jesus brought and embodied. The emphases that John's Gospel expresses bring out the points he wanted to make.

Jesus Is Messiah

John is unusual among the evangelists in that he indicates his purpose in writing his Gospel explicitly, in a brief paragraph that may well have been the concluding verses of what can consequently be regarded as the first edition of his Gospel:

> Now Jesus did many other signs in the presence of his disciples, which are not written in this book. But these are written so that you may come to believe that Jesus is the Christ, the Son of God, and that through believing you may have life in his name. (John 20:30–31)

A somewhat curious fact is that John is the only writer in the New Testament to use the Greek term *Messias* (John 1:41; 4:25), a transliteration of the Hebrew term "Messiah," rather than only the Greek translation, *Christos* (a term he uses regularly in his Gospel). The curiosity is that when the good news of Jesus had already been widely circulated in the wider gentile world and *Christos* had become in effect part of a proper name ("Jesus Christ"), it is the last of the New Testament Gospels that retains the Hebrew term with its titular sense.

As John 20:30–31 clearly implies, to bring out the significance of Jesus as the Messiah/Christ was one of John's chief concerns:

John 1:41	Andrew "first found his brother Simon [Peter] and said to him, 'We have found the Messiah' (which is translated Christ)."
John 4:25–26	The woman at the well said to Jesus, "'I know that Messiah is coming' (who is called Christ). 'When he comes, he will proclaim all things to us.' Jesus said to her, 'I am he.'"
John 7	A debate about Jesus's significance: the question being asked by the crowd, "Can it be that the authorities really know that this is the Christ?" (7:26), sparks off a debate that continues for the next two paragraphs (7:26–44).
John 9	The controversy provoked by Jesus's healing a blind man, including the response of the authorities who "agreed that anyone who confessed Jesus to be the Christ would be put out of the synagogue" (9:22).
John 10:24	"The Jews" ask, "How long will you keep us in suspense? If you are the Christ, tell us plainly" (see also 12:34).

John 11:27	Prior to the raising of her brother Lazarus, Martha confesses: "I believe that you are the Christ, the Son of God, the one coming into the world."

John 17:3	Also sums up John's intentions when he quotes Jesus as praying, "This is eternal life, that they may know you, the only true God, and Jesus Christ whom you have sent."

It is worth repeating that the author of the last of the Gospels in the New Testament still retains the titular sense of Christ/Messiah when, as we shall see more clearly later, Christ had become almost a proper name for Jesus ("Jesus Christ") when the titular significance of the name (the Christ or Messiah) had begun to fade. The loss of this titular significance can be easily understood since in the wider mission in predominantly gentile territory the Jewish significance of the title was less relevant and could readily have been neglected. But for John, still hoping to persuade his fellow Jews that Jesus was indeed the Messiah, it was still necessary to emphasize the significance of the title.

It is also worth noting that John does not hesitate to record that Jesus was hailed to be and recognized as "the king of Israel," even though Matthew and Mark recall the title being used only by the crowds mocking the crucified Jesus (Matt 27:42 // Mark 15:32).

John 1:49	"Nathanael replied, 'Rabbi, you are the Son of God! You are the King of Israel!'"

John 12:13	The crowds greet Jesus entering Jerusalem: "Hosanna! Blessed is the one who comes in the name of the Lord—the King of Israel." And John goes on to quote Zech 9:9: "Look, your king is coming, sitting on a donkey's colt!"

The interesting point is that "king of Israel" was a dangerously political title to be used of Jesus in a state controlled by the Romans.

John records Jesus's own hesitation at the thought of taking on such a role (John 6:15). But he does not hesitate to record that Jesus's trial before the Roman governor, Pilate, focused on whether Jesus was "the king of the Jews" (John 18:33–39). John also reports that Jesus was abused by the soldiers as "king of the Jews" (John 19:3), and that the title that the crucified Jesus bore was an issue between Pilate and the chief priests (John 19:12–22). The one qualification that John makes is to record Jesus as responding to Pilate: "My kingdom is not from this world. If my kingdom were from this world, my followers would be fighting to keep me from being handed over to the Jews. But as it is, my kingdom is not from here" (John 18:36). This tension between "king of Israel" and "kingdom of God" (John 3:3, 5; the only other "kingdom" reference in John) is relatively minor in the Fourth Gospel, but it is nonetheless of significance and may hint at how John's community coped with the destruction of "the kingdom of Israel" in the latter decades of the first century.

It is even more striking in John's presentation that Jesus is shown as fulfilling and in effect superseding other central features of Israel's history and religion.

John 1:17	"The law indeed was given through Moses; grace and truth came through Jesus Christ."
John 1:29	"Here is the Lamb of God who takes away the sin of the world."
John 2:19–21	"Destroy this temple, and in three days I will raise it up." The author explains: "He was speaking of the temple of his body."
John 4:10–14	"Those who drink of the water that I will give them will never be thirsty."
John 6:48–58	"I am the bread of life. . . . The one who eats this bread will live forever."
John 8:58	"Very truly, I tell you, before Abraham was, I am."

John 15:1   Alluding to the familiar imagery of Israel as a
              vine or a vineyard, Jesus says, "I am the true
              vine, and my Father is the vinegrower."[2]

There is evidently a tension here—between Jesus as the one who fulfills Israel's expectations and also supersedes them. This presumably reflects the tensions within the Jesus movement in the late first century, which was confronted both by the destruction of Israel and of Israel's temple and by the increasing hostility of the Pharisees ("the [hostile] Jews" in John's terminology). Which way should the Jewish followers of Jesus turn? This was evidently the dilemma confronting the author of the Gospel of John. According to his own usage, there were still many of "the Jews" who were open to the claim that Jesus was the Messiah and to the claims of his followers—as his presentation makes clear.[3] Hence the main purpose of his Gospel, already noted in John 20:30-31, to persuade as many of the author's fellow Jews to join him in believing "that Jesus is the Christ, the Son of God," in the confidence of faith "that through believing [they] may have life in his name." John may well have anticipated that there would soon be a parting of the ways for the believing Jews, but the Jewishness of the Jesus movement was too fundamental for him to give up without a struggle.

Jesus Is the Son of God

One of the more remarkable features of John's Gospel is that Jesus refers to God as "Father" in it much more frequently than he does in the Synoptics. The statistics are striking: 3 times in Mark, 8 in Luke, 35 in Matthew, and 100 in John. Here are a few examples—all statements made by Jesus, and the references all unique to John:

John 2:16   Jesus protests in the temple: "Stop making my
              Father's house a marketplace!"

2. Ps 80:8-18; Isa 5:1-7; Jer 2:21; Ezek 15:1-5; 17:1-10; 19:10-15; Hos 10:1-2.
3. John 6:52; 7:11-12, 31, 35, 40-44; 10:19-21; 12:11, 17-19; 12:34.

John 5:37	"The Father who sent me has himself testified on my behalf."
John 6:44	"No one can come to me unless drawn by the Father who sent me."
John 8:54	"It is my Father who glorifies me, he of whom you say, 'He is our God.'"
John 10:30	"The Father and I are one."
John 15:1	"I am the true vine, and my Father is the vinegrower."

This is matched by John's references to Jesus as "the Son of God," again distinctive of John. For example:

John 1:34	John the Baptist says: "I myself have seen and have testified that this is the Son of God."
John 1:49	Nathanael hails Jesus: "Rabbi, you are the Son of God!"
John 10:36	Jesus asks "the Jews": "Can you say that the one whom the Father has sanctified and sent into the world is blaspheming because I said, 'I am God's Son'?"
John 11:27	Martha confesses: "I believe that you are the Messiah, the Son of God."

And we should recall that John's expressed intention was to bring his readers to belief that Jesus was not only the Christ, but "the Christ, the Son of God" (John 20:31). Here we should just add that John is the only evangelist to refer to Jesus as God's "one and only son" (*monogenēs*; John 1:14, 18; 3:16, 18).

Not least, the point of this for John was to emphasize that

Jesus's mission was authorized by the Father—again a distinctive Johannine emphasis:

John 3:17   "God did not send the Son into the world to condemn the world, but in order that the world might be saved through him."

John 3:35   "The Father loves the Son and has placed all things in his hands."

John 5:19   "The Son can do nothing on his own, but only what he sees the Father doing; for whatever the Father does, the Son does likewise."

John 5:26   "Just as the Father has life in himself, so he has granted the Son also to have life in himself."

John 6:38   "I have come . . . to do . . . the will of him who sent me."

John 12:50   "What I speak . . . I speak just as the Father has told me."[4]

Here again we see how John has adapted the tradition of Jesus's ministry. The earlier evangelists recall that the term "the Son of God" was used in Jesus's temptation (Matt 4:3, 6 // Luke 4:3, 9), by demoniacs (Mark 3:11 // Luke 4:41; Mark 5:7 parr.), by his disciples marveling at Jesus's walking on the water (Matt 14:33),[5] by the high priest at Jesus's trial (Matt 26:63 // Luke 22:70), by the crucified robber and the mocking officials (Matt 27:40, 43), and in fearful surprise by the centurion in charge of

---

4. Here we might note that John adds to the synoptic tradition of Jesus referring to himself as "the Son of Man" the thought of the Son of Man descending from heaven—"No one has ascended into heaven except the one who descended from heaven, the Son of Man" (John 3:13).

5. Matthew adds to Peter's confession at Caesarea Philippi, "You are the Christ" (Mark 8:29)—"You are the Christ, the Son of the living God" (Matt 16:16).

Jesus's crucifixion (Mark 15:39 // Matt 27:54). And from early days in the postresurrection mission the confession of Jesus to be "the Son of God" was a natural expression of earliest Christian faith.[6] So the obvious conclusion is that John's Gospel reflects this fuller faith and does not hesitate to depict Jesus as himself laying claim to the title—no longer simply a temptation to be misused, no longer a status just recognized by demoniacs, no longer a mission to be dismissed by Jewish authorities or crucified thieves, but a role recognized and affirmed by Jesus himself. This should not surprise us since it was precisely the conviction, not only that Jesus was God's Son, but also that in being able to echo Jesus's own prayer, "Abba! Father!," the earliest believers were affirming that they too were "children of God . . . heirs of God and joint heirs with Christ" (Rom 8:15–17). Here too, then, John's portrayal of Jesus shows how profound was the impact made by Jesus and how that impact reflected back on the way John remembered and portrayed Jesus.

Jesus Is the Divine Word

If John's elaboration of the claims that Jesus is Israel's long-expected Messiah, and is indeed the Son of God, was striking; even more so is the wholly new claim in the opening paragraph of the Gospel. The astonishing claim is that Jesus not only spoke the word of God, as had the prophets of old, but *was* the Word of God! It is one of the features of John's Gospel that immediately catches the attention—that John begins not with the first phase of Jesus's ministry (as had Mark), nor with his birth (as had Matthew and Luke), but with the Logos/Word as the divine agent or medium of creation. In his bolder reflections Paul had come close to this (as in Phil 2:6 and Col 2:9). It is only with John, however, that we see in precise words the concept of incarnation, of Jesus as the incarnation of God's creative agency specifically articulated as never before—and with an unexpected boldness in his opening words.

---

6. As in Rom 1:4; 2 Cor 1:19; Gal 2:20.

In the beginning was the Word, and the Word was with God, and the Word was God. He was in the beginning with God. All things came into being through him, and without him not one thing came into being. What has come into being in him was life, and the life was the light of all people. The light shines in the darkness, and the darkness did not overcome it. . . . He was in the world, and the world came into being through him. . . . He came to what was his own, and his own people did not accept him. But to all who received him, who believed in his name, he gave power to become children of God, who were born, not of blood or of the will of the flesh or of the will of man, but of God. And the Word became flesh and lived among us, and we have seen his glory, the glory of a father's only son, full of grace and truth. . . . From his fullness we have all received, grace upon grace. The law indeed was given through Moses; grace and truth came through Jesus Christ. No one has ever seen God. It is God the only Son, who is close to the Father's heart, who has made him known. (John 1:1–18)

It is hard for those who have been long familiar with this passage to appreciate just how exceptional it was when first written. The Word or Logos was of course familiar to both Jew and Greek. Those familiar with the Hebrew Bible would think, for example, of

Gen 15:1   "The word of the LORD came to Abram in a vision."

Ps 33:6   "By the word of the LORD the heavens were made, and all their host by the breath of his mouth."

And of course, they would think particularly of the prophets to whom "the word of the Lord came" on many occasions—as in

Isa 55:11   God says, "So shall my word be that goes out from my mouth; it shall not return to me empty, but it shall accomplish that which I purpose."

Jer 2:4   "Hear the word of the LORD, O house of Jacob."

For those more familiar with Greek thought, the idea of the *logos spermatikos*, the seed-logos, the creative energy behind the world, and seeded within the human individual, would be nothing new. For John it would no doubt have been familiar that *logos* could refer both to the word unexpressed and the word expressed. How better to use it than to underline the significance of Jesus: Jesus as the embodiment of the mind and intention of God, as *himself* expressing what hitherto had been expressed only in the words of the inspired prophet. What was only implicit in creation was now expressed clearly. In other words, John 1:14, "The Word became flesh and lived among us," was something totally unexpected and new, making a wholly mind-blowing claim: that Jesus, as God's Word, has expressed what was hitherto the inexpressible and has made the unknowable known.

We should not fail to note the significance of John's formulation in his claim that it is the Word of God that has been incarnated as Jesus. Not just the creative power of God. Not just the saving acts of God that have delivered Israel in the past, but the word of God, the creative and saving power of God in a rational form that would engage human intelligence and answer human puzzles and inquiries. The wonder of John 1:14 is that its claim engages the human readers and responds at every level of their being, the word-expressing mind not least.

Jesus Is the Divine Wisdom

Somewhat surprisingly, the thought of Jesus as the Word of God incarnate is not taken up or followed through in the rest of John's Gospel—suggesting to some that the prologue (John 1:1–18) was a later addition to the Gospel, perhaps in the second or third draft of the Gospel as composed by John or by the group around him. However, in Jewish thought there was a more familiar way of speaking of God's interaction with his creation and his people. This was the figure of divine Wisdom, familiar at the time of Jesus particularly in the wisdom literature of Israel's Scriptures.

Prov 3:19   "The LORD by wisdom founded the earth."

Prov 8:27, 30   Wisdom cries out: "When he established the heavens, I was there. . . . Then I was beside him, like a master worker."

Sir 24:1, 23   "Wisdom praises herself, and tells of her glory in the midst of her people. . . . All this is the book of the covenant of the Most High God, the law that Moses commanded us."

Bar 3:9–4:2   "Hear the commandments of life, O Israel; give ear, and learn wisdom. . . . She [Wisdom] is the book of the commandments of God, the law that endures forever. All who hold her fast will live, and those who forsake her will die. Turn, O Jacob, and take her; walk toward the shining of her light."

The point should not be missed, that the incarnation of Wisdom in the flesh of Jesus was foreshadowed by the embodiment of Wisdom in "the book of the covenant" with Israel, "the commandments of God."

In John there are many echoes of what was said of Wisdom. For example:

Wis 9:17–18   "Who has learned your counsel, unless you have given wisdom and sent your holy spirit from on high? And thus . . . people . . . were saved by wisdom."

John 3:16–17   "God so loved the world that he gave his only Son." He sent his Son into the world "in order that the world might be saved through him."

Sir 15:3	"She [Wisdom] will feed him with the bread of learning, and give him the water of wisdom to drink."
Sir 24:21	"Those who eat of me will hunger for more, and those who drink of me will thirst for more."
John 4:14	Jesus says to the woman at the well, "Those who drink of the water that I will give them will never be thirsty. The water that I will give will become in them a spring of water gushing up to eternal life."
Prov 9:5	Wisdom's invitation: "Come, eat of my bread and drink of the wine I have mixed."
Sir 15:3	"She [Wisdom] will feed him with the bread of learning, and give him the water of wisdom to drink."
John 6:35	Jesus says, "I am the bread of life. Whoever comes to me will never be hungry, and whoever believes in me will never be thirsty."

A striking feature should not be ignored. In Jewish thought the figure of Wisdom was feminine, the Jews realizing from early on that the divine could not be limited to a single gender. The creative power of God, expressed above all in the human species, cannot be restricted to one form of that species. "God created humankind in his image . . . male and female he created them" (Gen 1:27). "Male and female" is the image of God. So there is no problem in John expressing the incarnation in female terms. The incarnation embodies the creative energy of God in creating male and female. The claim made in John 1:14 could be equally made in terms of Wisdom: "Wisdom became flesh" in and as Jesus. John could hardly have been bolder in his claim that everything the Jewish writers of the Hebrew Bible tried to express by their talk of the Word of

God and the Wisdom of God had been summed up in Jesus, the incarnate Word, the incarnate Wisdom of God.

Other Characteristic Emphases

John's creative boldness in his presentation of Jesus was not limited to his Christology. The incarnate self-expression of God embodied a revelation of God and from God that had some very important corollaries for John and for the readers of his Gospel.

The New Commandment

John 13:34–35	"I give you a new commandment, that you love one another. Just as I have loved you, you also should love one another. By this everyone will know that you are my disciples, if you have love for one another."
John 14:21	"They who have my commandments and keep them are those who love me; and those who love me will be loved by my Father, and I will love them and reveal myself to them."
John 15:10	"If you keep my commandments, you will abide in my love, just as I have kept my Father's commandments and abide in his love."
John 15:12–13	"This is my commandment, that you love one another as I have loved you. No one has greater love than this, to lay down one's life for one's friends."

It should be noted that Jesus does not hesitate to speak of his love as conditional. The experience of being loved was not to provide a cozy embrace that could compensate for the world's rejection or hate. The experience of being loved by Jesus would generate love for one another and express itself in keeping Christ's commandments. Here the thought of "love of neighbor" is focused in love of fellow believer—probably a reflection of a community under increasingly hostile pressure.

Individualism

Another notable emphasis in John's Gospel is his individualism, focused once again on Jesus. The shepherd calls each sheep by name (John 10:3–4). Each branch abides in Jesus the vine, tended by his Father the vinegrower (John 15:1–7). Each munches the flesh of the Son of Man and drinks his blood (John 6:53–58). Most striking is the invitation of Jesus in John 7:37–38: "Let anyone who is thirsty come to me, and let the one who believes in me drink. As the Scripture has said, 'Out of the believer's heart shall flow rivers of living water.'" Which Scripture was in mind at this point is disputed. It may indeed be that the evangelist had in mind various scriptural passages, including the water miraculously provided for the Israelites in the wilderness from the rock (Exod 17:1–6), which Paul referred to as "the spiritual rock" identified with Christ (1 Cor 10:4). John may also have had in mind Ezekiel's vision of the temple from which flowed the living water (Ezek 47:1–11), a vision taken up also by other prophets.[7] The power of the imagery in a land well used to drought should not be missed—not least the ambiguity of whether the heart from which flows the living water is that of Christ or of the one who believes in Christ and drinks from the water flowing from Christ.

Worship in Spirit and Truth

A further point worth noting in John's Gospel is that he does not hesitate to show Jesus speaking of worship as no longer tied to a

---

7. Isa 43:19–20; Joel 3:18; and Zech 14:8.

cultic center but as a worship in spirit and truth. Jesus, speaking to the Samaritan woman at the well on the subject of worship and on the question whether valid worship could be offered only in Jerusalem, affirms his Jewish heritage. But then he adds: "The hour is coming, and is now here, when the true worshipers will worship the Father in spirit and truth, for the Father seeks such as these to worship him. God is spirit, and those who worship him must worship in spirit and truth" (John 4:23–24). Bearing in mind that John's Gospel was written in the post-70 period, that is, after the destruction of the Jerusalem temple by the Romans, and that Jesus had already transferred attention from the temple to himself (John 2:19–21), the words to the woman at the well strongly suggest that the Johannine believers were finding in these words attributed to Jesus the answer to the despair that the destruction of Jerusalem and its temple must have caused to so many.

Silences in John

Another interesting feature of John's Gospel is what he does not say or mention. For example, there is no mention in John of apostles, prophets, or teachers. Rather, we find Jesus speaking thus:

John 6:45	"It is written in the prophets, 'And they shall all be taught by God'" (Isa 54:13).
John 14:26	"The Advocate, the Holy Spirit, whom the Father will send in my name, will teach you everything, and remind you of all that I have said to you."

What does that tell us about the pattern of Christianity and of Christian worship and leadership that John espoused?

John's Silence about Baptism and the Lord's Supper

Again, we find in John's Gospel no mention of Jesus's baptism and no mention of the Last Supper. To be sure, one of Jesus's extended sermons in John is the great bread of life discourse. Thus John recalls Jesus as saying, "Those who eat my flesh and drink my blood have eternal life; . . . for my flesh is true food and my blood is true drink" (John 6:54–55). That would seem to be John's equivalent to the Last Supper and presumably reflects how the Johannine church or churches saw their sharing of the eucharistic bread and wine. But then John has Jesus concluding with the warning not to put a misplaced emphasis on the bread and wine: "It is the spirit that gives life; the flesh is useless. The words that I have spoken to you are spirit and life" (John 6:63).

One can hardly help contrasting this with the theology of Ignatius, writing only about twenty years later. Ignatius seems to be going in almost the opposite direction from John in his insistence on the centrality of the Eucharist and in his attempts to reinforce the authority of local bishops. His letter to the Smyrnaeans is typical of his exhortations. In *Smyrnaeans* 7.1–8.2, Ignatius criticizes his opponents:

> They abstain from the Eucharist and prayer, since they do not confess that the Eucharist is the flesh of our Savior Jesus Christ. . . . It is fitting to avoid such people and not even to speak to them, either privately or in public. . . . All of you should follow the bishop as Jesus Christ follows the Father. . . . Let no one do anything involving the church without the bishop. . . . Let the congregation be wherever the bishop is; just as wherever Jesus Christ is, there also is the universal church. It is not permitted either to baptize or to hold a love feast without the bishop. But whatever he approves is acceptable to God, so that everything you do should be secure and valid.[8]

8. *The Apostolic Fathers*, trans. Bart Ehrman, 2 vols., Loeb Classical Library (Cambridge, MA: Harvard University Press, 2003).

Ignatius, of course, was mapping out the way ahead for the main body of Christianity. But it is quite hard to avoid the impression that John was reacting to and protesting against the kind of developments that only a few years later become apparent in Ignatius. That is, if John's Gospel was finally formulated in Ephesus, in the Asia Minor through which Ignatius was to pass less than a generation later, then it is quite likely that John was in effect protesting against the ecclesiology and sacramental theology that Ignatius was to promote so vigorously not long afterward. This is why John's Gospel, with its lack of reference to formally appointed church leaders, its passing over Jesus's baptism and Last Supper, and its warning against misinterpreting Jesus's identification of himself as the bread of life, has sometimes been categorized as a kind of conventicle Christianity—in effect a protest against the developments that Ignatius was to advocate. Here it may be significant that while Ignatius certainly knew and echoed the synoptic tradition on several occasions, it is much less clear that he knew and regarded highly the Johannine tradition. Were they set on alternative forms of earliest Christianity? This is a question worth asking, even when we recall that John was included in the canon of the New Testament and Ignatius was not.

*   *   *

In the light of what we have just noted, it is quite hard to avoid the question: Did John go too far? Even more serious is the fact that John seems to have appealed more to gnostics than he did to others. Gnosticism made a sharp distinction between flesh and spirit, so that the Johannine Christ was very appealing to them. It was not difficult for them to see the Johannine Christ in docetic terms, that is, the belief that Jesus only *appeared* in the flesh, *seemed* to be flesh.[9] Indeed, the first commentary that we know to have been written on the Gospel of John was by Heracleon, a Valentinian.[10] So much indeed was the Fourth Gospel capable of

9. *Docet*, Latin for "it seems." See also ch. 8 below on 1–3 John.
10. Valentinus (c. 100–160 CE) was the best known and most successful

being identified with a gnostic standpoint that the Alogi (second half of the second century) and the Roman presbyter Caius (early third century) both ascribed John's Gospel to the gnostic Cerinthus. It was Irenaeus, toward the end of the second century, who rescued John for orthodoxy, so that from the third century onward John became increasingly the sourcebook and scriptural keystone of orthodox Christology.[11]

The debate, however, was not settled, and in the second half of the nineteenth century it was revived. Most notably the famous New Testament theologian Rudolf Bultmann argued that the Fourth Gospel drew on an early form of gnostic thought, again raising the question: Did John overemphasize Jesus's divinity and play down his humanity? The answer in fact is No! The emphasis in John 1:14 is clear:

> The Word *became flesh* and lived among us,
> and we have seen his glory,
> the glory as of a father's only son,
> full of grace and truth.

It was the "became flesh" that the gnostics could not stomach. For them the antithesis between flesh and spirit was too sharp; it was unbridgeable. But this is precisely what John claims: the Word *became* flesh. In other words, he makes a clear and explicit assertion of the historicity and reality of the incarnation. And the way in which he brought out the central significance of Jesus's death was in effect making the same point: the incarnate Logos did not

---

early Christian gnostic theologian. According to Tertullian, he was a candidate for bishop of Rome, but when someone else was chosen he started his own group. He taught that there were three kinds of people, spiritual, psychical, and material, and that only those of a spiritual nature (his own followers) received the *gnosis* (knowledge) that allowed them to return to the divine fullness. Those of a psychic nature (ordinary Christians) would attain a lesser form of salvation, and those of a material nature (pagans and Jews) were doomed to perish.

11. See J. N. Sanders, *The Fourth Gospel in the Early Church: Its Origin and Influence on Christian Theology up to Irenaeus* (Cambridge: Cambridge University Press, 1943).

merely *appear* in flesh, but *became* flesh; and he did not just re-ascend to heaven, he first died, really died! In other words, John did not yield the vital ground to those who wished to increase the gospel's appeal to dualists who thought that flesh and spirit were irreconcilable. In complete contrast, he set out to preserve his Gospel precisely from the danger of a gnostic interpretation. The very points that docetism sought to deny are precisely the points that John sought to affirm: the reality of the eternal Word's becoming flesh, and the reality of his death.[12]

The fact that John was preserved and became a part of the canon of the New Testament indicates that the early church recognized the importance of reexpressing the good news to reach others outside the normal circles of Judaism. John indeed shows that one must be prepared to take some risks to ensure that the gospel is heard to speak to all conditions and all situations in a world very different from the Mediterranean world of the first century. So it remains a very relevant issue, today as then: Who is the best precedent for today—the Synoptics or John?

12. The issue is fought more fiercely in the Johannine letters. See ch. 8 below.

CHAPTER FOUR

Jesus according to

Acts

I n contrast to the Gospels, Jesus appears in Acts hardly at all. Acts 1:1–5 introduces Luke's second volume with a brief account of Jesus after his resurrection, appearing to his disciples, instructing them and "speaking about the kingdom of God" (Acts 1:2–3). More to the immediate point, Jesus tells them to wait in Jerusalem for the promise of the Holy Spirit, repeating the Baptist's promise that they would be baptized with the Holy Spirit (Acts 1:5). Surprisingly, the disciples ask whether the kingdom is to be restored to Israel (Acts 1:6)—Luke perhaps making the point that the disciples needed not only Jesus's resurrection but also the gift of the Spirit (Pentecost) to transform their thinking. In response, Jesus sidesteps the question and commissions the disciples to be his witnesses "in Jerusalem, in all Judea and Samaria, and to the ends of the earth" (Acts 1:7–8)—the agenda that Luke will follow in the rest of Acts. This is immediately followed by Jesus's ascension, with the angelic promise that Jesus would come back in the same way (Acts 1:9–11).

Then in effect Jesus disappears from the scene, although much talked about and preached by Peter and the others. He appears in the vision given to Stephen just before the latter's execution by stoning (Acts 7:55–56). Otherwise Jesus appears again only in reference to Paul. First in the conversion of Saul/Paul, but including the commission of Ananias to minister to him (Acts 9:10–16).

It is interesting to note that Luke was quite content to record the recollection of Paul's conversion in varied terms, twice, according to Luke, by Paul himself:

Acts 9:4–6   "He fell to the ground and heard a voice saying to him, 'Saul, Saul, why do you persecute me?' He [Saul] asked, 'Who are you, Lord?' The reply came, 'I am Jesus, whom you are persecuting. But get up and enter the city, and you will be told what you are to do.'"

Acts 22:7–8   More or less the same, but continuing with Saul asking what he should do. He is told to go into Damascus, where further instruction would be given.

Acts 26:14–18   Again the same question asked, with the addition, "It hurts you to kick against the goads," and with a much fuller commission then and there to take the good news of Jesus to the gentiles.

It is interesting to compare the commission of Paul with the commission of Peter. Rather strikingly the great breakthrough in Peter's realization that the gospel was for non-Jews as well (Acts 10–11) is attributed *not* to a vision of Jesus but simply to a vision with an unidentified voice from heaven.[1] Likewise with Cornelius—who is given the vision of an angel (Acts 10:3–7, 30–32). Note also Peter's miraculous release from Herod's prison, attributed to "an angel of the Lord" (Acts 12:7–11). To be sure, Paul's breakthrough in taking his mission to Europe is inspired by a later vision of "a man of Macedonia" (Luke?) calling on him to "come over to Macedonia and help us" (Acts 16:9–10). But Paul also recalls a warning vision of Jesus early in his ministry (Acts 22:17–19), and for Paul there are later visions of the Lord confirming his success in Corinth (Acts 18:9) and reassuring him that he will bear witness also in Rome (Acts 23:11).

1. Acts 10:11–13, 15–17, 19; 11:5–9—"a voice."

The contrast between Peter and Paul at this point is notable, perhaps suggesting not only Luke's greater personal knowledge of Paul, but also his own conviction, and his desire to express this conviction, that the greater mission to the gentiles was truly inspired by Christ.

Also notable in Luke's narrative is how quickly "the name of Jesus/the Lord/Christ" becomes a feature. The first mention of what can be called Christian baptism comes at the end of Peter's Pentecost sermon: it is already established that those who respond to his message should "be baptized . . . in the name of Jesus Christ" (Acts 2:38). The lame man is restored to fitness "in/by the name of Jesus Christ" (Acts 3:6; 4:10). In response the "rulers, elders, and scribes," together with Annas the high priest "and all who were of the high-priestly family" (Acts 4:5–6), charge the disciples "not to speak or teach . . . in the name of Jesus" (Acts 4:18; 5:40). Philip proclaims the good news of the kingdom of God to Samaritans, and many are "baptized in the name of the Lord Jesus" (Acts 8:12, 16). The converted Saul preaches in Jerusalem, "speaking boldly in the name of the Lord" (Acts 9:27–28). All that is clear and consistent.

Rather unclear, however, is the weight that should be given to the title "Lord" when applied to Jesus. As already noted, the problem is that at one end of the range of meaning "the Lord" is a way of speaking of God. But at the other end it is a polite form of address to someone higher up the spectrum of social prestige.[2] So, always close to hand when the title is used of someone is the question as to where in the range of meaning this usage should be placed. The issue, already mentioned in chapter 2 above, is posed by Peter when, in claiming that God had raised Jesus from the dead and exalted him to heaven, he cites Psalm 110:1: "The Lord said to my Lord, 'Sit at my right hand, until I make your enemies your footstool.'" From which he immediately concludes that "God has made him both Lord and Christ, this Jesus whom you crucified" (Acts 2:34–36). "My Lord" in Psalm 110:1 presumably refers to the king, so the application to Jesus, who is "exalted at the right hand of God" (2:33), is certainly well toward the high end of the spectrum, as Acts 2:36 implies, "both Lord and Christ." And "the

2. E.g., in Matt 8:2, 6, 8; 9:28; Luke 9:59, 61; 10:40; 11:1.

Lord Jesus (Christ)" is a regular reference in Acts;[3] for example, Stephen prays to the Lord Jesus (Acts 7:59–60), Saul breathes out "threats and murder against the disciples of the Lord" (Acts 9:1), Peter proclaims to Cornelius that "he [Jesus Christ] is Lord of all" (Acts 10:36), and Paul and Barnabas entrust the converts in Antioch "to the Lord in whom they had come to believe" (Acts 14:23).

One of the most striking passages in Acts is when Paul and Barnabas are on mission through Asia Minor, uncertain where to go next. They had been "forbidden by the Holy Spirit to speak the word in Asia." But when "they attempted to go into Bithynia," "the Spirit of Jesus did not allow them" (Acts 16:6–7). "The Spirit of Jesus" is a very unusual phrase, paralleled only by Philippians 1:19, where Paul speaks of the assistance/support of "the Spirit of Jesus Christ" sustaining him through his time of trial.[4] Clearly in both passages the conviction was strong not only that the power that inspired Paul's mission was the same power that had inspired Jesus's mission, but also that that power had demonstrated or even taken its character from Jesus and his mission. Theirs was a continuation of the same mission. The Spirit that inspired Paul and Barnabas had inspired Jesus, and the character of Jesus's mission showed the character of the Spirit that inspired their mission. It was presumably in this way that the Christian understanding of God as Trinity came to expression—the conviction that Jesus was not only inspired by God's Spirit but also so demonstrated the character of the Spirit that the Spirit could be referred to quite naturally as "the Spirit of Jesus."

The Sermons in Acts

As interesting as the Lukan narrative is regarding the developing Christology of the first Christians, the most interesting developments in the earliest understanding of Jesus are evident in the

---

3. Acts 4:33; 8:16; 9:17; 11:17, 20; 15:11, 26; 16:31; 19:5, 13, 17; 20:21, 24, 35; 21:13.

4. "The Spirit of Christ" is a phrase used also in Rom 8:9 and 1 Pet 1:11. In the former passage it is quite obvious that "the Spirit of Christ" is another way of referring to "the Spirit of God."

speeches and sermons, one of the most notable features in Acts. There are many brief references to conversations and brief exchanges, but the sermons stand out:

Acts 2:14–36/39	Peter's sermon on the day of Pentecost
Acts 3:11–26	Peter's sermon in Solomon's Portico
Acts 4:8–12	Peter's answer to charges before the Jerusalem council
Acts 4:24–30	Jerusalem believers' response to the release of Peter and John
Acts 7:2–53	Stephen's defense speech before the Jerusalem council
Acts 8:30–35	Philip bearing witness to the Ethiopian eunuch
Acts 10:34–43	Peter's exposition to Cornelius and friends
Acts 11:4–18	Peter's explanation of his actions in Jerusalem
Acts 13:16–41	Paul's preaching in Pisidian Antioch
Acts 15:13–21	James's defense of the turn to the gentiles
Acts 15:23–29	The Jerusalem church's message to the new churches
Acts 17:22–31	Paul's sermon in Athens
Acts 20:17–35	Paul's parting speech in Miletus
Acts 22:1–21	Paul's first defense speech in Jerusalem
Acts 24:10–21	Paul's defense before the Roman governor Felix

Acts 26:2–29   Paul's defense before King Agrippa

Acts 28:25–28   Paul's final statement in Rome

As with all speeches attested in ancient literature, there is a question whether they are a true record of what was actually said on the occasion or simply the work of the author's imagination.[5] It is indeed likely that Luke has crafted his record in accordance with the common practice of the day. This no doubt is indicated by the relative brevity of the speeches, which would take only a few minutes to deliver. Indeed, they are better regarded as cameos, finely crafted miniatures, rather than outlines or abbreviations. At the same time, however, in most cases there is an individuality and distinctiveness of material used, which points to the conclusion that *Luke has been able to draw on and incorporate tradition*—not necessarily any record or specific recollection as such, but tradition related to and, in Luke's considered judgment, representative of the individual's views and well suited to the occasion.[6] In fact, the speeches of Acts show clear indications of non-Lukan material, which was presumably the result of his investigations and therefore probably provides source material for earliest Christian proclamation and teaching, but only if used with care. They represent Luke's impression of the episodes and characters he describes, though it is history and theology seen through Luke's eyes and reflecting also his own concerns.

5. Much quoted in discussions on this question are the words of the Greek historian Thucydides, often regarded as the greatest of ancient historians: "As to the speeches that were made either before or during the war, it was hard for me, and for others who reported them to me, to recollect the exact words. I have therefore put into the mouth of each speaker the sentiments proper to the occasion, expressed as I thought he would be likely to express them, while at the same time I endeavored, as nearly as I could, to give the general import of what was actually said" (*History of the Peloponnesian War* 1.22.1; Benjamin Jowett, *Thucydides: Translated into English*, 2 vols., 2nd ed. [Oxford: Clarendon, 1900]).

6. Luke's own claims regarding his two-volume work should be given due respect: "I too decided, after investigating everything carefully from the very first, to write an orderly account" (Luke 1:3).

I give as two examples Peter's speech on the initiating day of Pentecost (Acts 2:14–36/39) and his sermon to Cornelius, the Roman centurion (Acts 10:34–43).

Peter's Pentecost Speech (Acts 2:14–36/39)

There are several indications here that Luke was able to draw on earlier tradition. The speech is a good example of a Jewish sermon—a midrash on Joel 2:28–32, with supporting texts from the Psalms, and with Acts 2:39 (alluding again to Joel) rounding it off. The eschatology is surprisingly primitive as compared with the rest of Acts. It is generally reckoned that Luke himself pulls back from the belief that the coming (again) of Christ was imminent: he seems to qualify such expectation elsewhere;[7] and in the perspective of Acts the church seems to be set for a long haul, with an eschatology of "the last things" rather than of expectation that "the end is nigh."[8] So it is noteworthy that Peter's speech retains that primitive note of imminent expectation: the quotation from Joel replaces the Hebrew "afterwards" by the much more pregnant "in the last days" (Acts 2:17);[9] and Acts 2:19–20 retains the apocalyptic imagery of cosmic convulsion that heightens the expectation. The impression given by the passage, that "the great and terrible day of the Lord" (the day of judgment) was imminent, again indicates very early tradition.

Not least, the Christology itself seems primitive at a number of points. The personal name, "Jesus the Nazarene" (Acts 2:22), "Jesus" (2:32), "this Jesus" (2:36), is quickly lost elsewhere in the New Testament behind the more formal "Christ" or "Lord." Jesus is described in remarkably undivine language as "a man attested to you by God," his success spoken of in terms of "signs that God did through him" (2:22). "The Messiah" is still a title (2:31), whereas

---

7. Notably Luke 19:11; 21:24; Acts 1:6–7.

8. Note, e.g., that the threat of final judgment seems less urgent in Acts 10:42 and 17:31.

9. Cf. Isa 2:2; Mic 4:1.

elsewhere in the New Testament it has become more or less a proper name, "Jesus Christ." Quite remarkable is the depiction of Jesus as the bestower of the Spirit, consequent upon his exaltation (2:33)—an expectation that probably reflects the influence of Jesus's predecessor, John the Baptist,[10] but that hardly appears elsewhere in the New Testament. In some ways most striking of all, the resurrection/ascension is cited as evidence that "God has made him both Lord and Messiah" (2:36). Such an affirmation was quite likely in the first flush of enthusiasm, but the implication that Jesus was only *made* Messiah at his resurrection was soon excluded by more carefully worded formulations.[11] Given that at the period of Luke's writing, Christology was much more developed, it must be judged unlikely that Luke was attempting to promote these emphases. It is much more likely that he drew them from traditions or memories that his inquiry (or common knowledge) had brought to light.

The conclusion seems clear, then. However much Peter's first sermon owes to Luke's compositional technique, it is very likely that he was able to draw on very early sources for his composition. It remains unlikely that any initial preaching would have been so brief. But it is not an outline or a summary: it contains a complete and rounded argument. Consequently we may imagine Luke carefully inquiring of those who remembered the earliest preaching of the Jerusalem church, and crafting the sermon from these memories and from emphases that had lasted from the earliest period of Christianity's beginnings in Jerusalem to his own day.

Peter's Address to Cornelius (Acts 10:34–43)

The sermon of Peter falls in the second half of the story of the conversion of the gentile centurion Cornelius. As usual, it is a fine Lukan cameo; it would take little more than a minute to deliver. Acts 10:44 suggests, and Acts 11:15 states explicitly, that the speech

10. Mark 1:8 parr.; cf. Acts 1:5.
11. But cf. Acts 13:33; Heb 1:5; 5:5.

had hardly started when the Spirit intervened. But, as usual with the Lukan speech cameos, this one is a nicely rounded whole, where nothing more need be said.

The structure is clear enough. The main body of the speech (Acts 10:36–43) is built round five scriptural allusions:

Acts 10:34—Deut 10:17:	God is not partial, a fundamental principle of Jewish justice, often echoed in early Jewish literature.[12]
Acts 10:36—Ps 107:20:	"He sent out his word and healed them."
Acts 10:36—Isa 52:7 (less clear):	"Those who preach peace." Both texts in Acts 10:36 may well have belonged to an early arsenal of Christian texts: Ps 107:20 is echoed again in Acts 13:26, and Isa 52:7 is cited in Rom 10:15 as part of a catena of texts.
Acts 10:38—Isa 61:1:	"Anointed with the Holy Spirit."
Acts 10:39—Deut 21:22:	"Hanged on a tree." That this was part of early polemic against belief in a crucified Messiah may be implied by Gal 3:13—"Cursed is everyone who hangs on a tree" (cf. 1 Cor 1:23). This polemic was possibly part of Paul's motivation as a persecutor. Such a play on Deuteronomy is not developed elsewhere.

12. 2 Chr 19:7; Sir 35:12–13; Jubilees 5:16; 21:4; 30:16; 33:18; 1 Enoch 63:8; Psalms of Solomon 2:18; Pseudo-Philo 20:4; 2 Baruch 13:8, 44:4; as also Paul (Rom 2:11).

These are followed by the familiar rehearsal of Jesus's death and resurrection, and an implicit call for belief and promise of forgiveness. It contains the same Lukan, but also possibly older, features: Jewish responsibility for Jesus's execution (Acts 10:39); the theme of witness thrice repeated (Acts 10:39, 41, 43); the resurrection as something "manifest" (Acts 10:40, 41); the mention of Jesus's name (Acts 10:43); but now also a more distant, less urgent eschatology (Acts 10:42), suggestive of a longer time perspective.

But once again there are primitive features:

1. The Israel-centeredness of the message (Acts 10:36, 42).[13]
2. "You know," perhaps implying a Judean audience (Acts 10:36).
3. The setting of John the Baptist and his baptism at and as the beginning of Jesus's mission (Acts 10:37; cf. 1:22; 13:24).
4. Jesus is identified as "the one from Nazareth" (Acts 10:38), still needing to be identified, a more weighty title not yet assumed (cf. 2:22).
5. God anointed him with the Spirit and power (Acts 10:38). In other words, he is presented as an inspired prophet—a primitive Christology. The echo of Isaiah 61:1 may reflect Jesus's own self-understanding as implied in Luke 6:20 and 7:22, but is not characteristic of the heightened Christology of the second generation.
6. Jesus's mission of healing is described in restrained terms (good deeds and exorcisms), and his success is again attributed to the fact that "God was with him" (Acts 10:38; cf. 2:22). The description is one that might have come from the mouth of any sympathetic observer of Jesus's ministry. The juxtaposition of this very moderate portrayal of Jesus with the final confessional claim of Acts 10:36 ("He is Lord of all") is striking.
7. The suffering-reversal theme—they put him to death, but God raised him (Acts 10:39-40)—not yet a doctrine of atonement. "On the third day" (Acts 10:40) is unparalleled in Acts, but is

13. Cf. Acts 3:25.

already enshrined in the early confessional formula received by Paul after his conversion (1 Cor 15:4).

8. That Jesus had been appointed "judge of the living and the dead" is a distinctive feature. It could be early: that God had chosen to give others a share in his role as final judge is reflected in Jewish speculation of the period in regard to such great heroes as Enoch and Abel,[14] as well as in very early Christian tradition (Luke 22:30; 1 Cor 6:2); and the identification of Jesus with the man-like figure ("one like a son of man") in the vision of Daniel 7:13–14 would have reinforced the link in the case of Jesus. On the other hand, the formulation is remarkably lacking in any sense of urgency (so also Acts 17:31; contrast Acts 3:19–20), and reads more like a doctrine of the last things framed in the light of Jesus's return having been much delayed.[15]

9. The scriptural allusions noted above, around which the speech has been molded, all appear early in Christian reflection about Jesus and his death, and are not characteristic of the heightened Christology of subsequent years.

In addition, Acts 10:34–35 looks like an introduction added to already existing material to fit it to the context: the jump from Acts 10:35 to 36 is rather abrupt ("You know the message he sent . . ."). It is possible, indeed, that verses 34–35 and 43 have been added to an already fairly coherent torso.

One plausible hypothesis that takes all the above details into account is that Luke has molded his cameo on some tradition of early preaching to gentile Godfearers. This would explain the slight tension between the more traditional formulations and the more universal dimension evident in Acts 10:34–35, 36c, 39 ("in Judea and in Jerusalem"), and 10:43 ("everyone who believes"). At all events, it does appear as though Luke has again followed Thucydides's practice of putting "into the mouth of each speaker

---

14. Jubilees 4:17–24; 1 Enoch 12–16; Testament of Abraham (A) 13:3–10; Testament of Abraham (B) 10; 11:2; 2 Enoch 22:8; 11QMelch 13–14.

15. But cf. 1 Pet 4:5 and 2 Tim 4:1.

the sentiments proper to the occasion," expressed as he thought the speaker would be likely to express them, while at the same time he endeavored, as nearly as he could, "to give the general import of what was actually said."

Without going into a lengthy examination of all the speeches in Acts, we can infer from the brief examination of these two that they provide a valuable testimony to what the first disciples believed, preached, and taught in the earliest days of Christianity. How did Luke gain access to such material? He probably did not see written versions of these speeches; that would imply a literary society and environment that is wholly unlikely for the beginnings of Christianity. But in the oral society, which we must envisage for the earliest Christian groups and communities, it is readily and appropriately possible to envisage the speeches, sermons, and teaching of leading figures (the apostles) providing material, themes and emphases, claims and arguments, which were taken up by those who emerged as teachers and elders of the individual groups and communities in their own preaching and teaching. Many of these emphases and arguments would have been superseded by further reflection and instruction within these communities and as the movement they represented spread and developed. We have seen some examples in the two sermons attributed to Peter. But Luke would have had little difficulty in finding older teachers and elders who could still recall these emphases and arguments of earlier days, even though the living tradition of the churches had now left them behind. Consequently we should not be embarrassed at the claim that the speeches in Acts give a good historical insight into the earliest Christian beliefs regarding Jesus.

Jesus according to the Sermons in Acts

So, what are the distinctive features in the way Acts presents Jesus in the sermons Luke has recorded?

Proclaiming the Resurrection of Jesus

Whereas Jesus proclaimed the kingdom of God, the sermons in Acts *proclaim Jesus*. Jesus has become the content of the message; the proclaimer has become the proclaimed. In particular, *the principal focus falls on the resurrection of Jesus*. Again and again it forms the central thrust of the message, both to Jew and to gentile:

Acts 2:14–36	Peter before the Jerusalem crowd: "God raised him up, having freed him from death. . . . This Jesus God raised up, and of that all of us are witnesses" (esp. 2:24–32).
Acts 3:12–26	And again: "You killed the Author of life, whom God raised from the dead. To this we are witnesses. . . . When God raised up his servant, he sent him first to you, to bless you."
Acts 4:1–2	The temple authorities were "much annoyed because they [Peter and John] were teaching the people and proclaiming that in Jesus there is the resurrection of the dead."
Acts 4:10–11	Peter testifying before the Jerusalem council: "This man is standing before you in good health by the name of Jesus Christ of Nazareth, whom you crucified, whom God raised from the dead."
Acts 4:33	"With great power the apostles gave their testimony to the resurrection of the Lord Jesus."
Acts 5:30	Peter again before the Jerusalem council: "The God of our ancestors raised up Jesus, whom you had killed by hanging him on a tree."
Acts 10:39–40	Peter preaching to the Roman centurion Cornelius: "They put him to death by hanging him on

a tree; but God raised him on the third day and allowed him to appear . . . to us who were chosen by God as witnesses."

Acts 13:29–37   Paul preaching in Pisidian Antioch: "They took him down from the tree and laid him in a tomb. But God raised him from the dead. . . . What God promised to our ancestors he has fulfilled for us, their children, by raising Jesus." Paul goes on to cite Ps 2:7, Isa 55:3, and Ps 15:10.

Acts 17:18   Some Athenians thought Paul was "a proclaimer of foreign divinities . . . because he was telling them the good news about Jesus and the resurrection."

Acts 17:31   Paul preaching to the Areopagus in Athens: "[God] has fixed a day on which he will have the world judged in righteousness by a man whom he has appointed, and of this he has given assurance to all by raising him from the dead."

Acts 24:21   Paul making self-defense before the Roman governor Felix in Jerusalem: "It is about the resurrection of the dead that I am on trial before you today."

This is all the more striking since in the Acts sermons hardly any concern is shown for the preresurrection ministry of Jesus; the only references are in Acts 2:22 and 10:36–39. More striking still, the actual sermons in Acts contain remarkably few echoes of Jesus's own message and teaching.[16] It is not an idle question, therefore, to ask: "What is the continuity between Jesus's proclamation of the kingdom and the proclamation in Acts of the resurrection of Jesus?"

16. Cf., however, the references to "the kingdom of God" (8:12; 14:22; 19:8; 20:25; 28:23, 31; also 20:35).

Absence of Theology about the Death of Jesus

An important corollary to the concentration in Acts on Jesus's resurrection is the absence of any theology regarding *the death of Jesus*. His death is mentioned, of course, but only as a bare fact (usually highlighting Jewish responsibility). The historical fact, however, is not interpreted.[17] It is never said, for example, that "Jesus died on our behalf," or "for our sins." There are no suggestions that Jesus's death was a sacrifice. The few brief allusions to Jesus as the Servant (of Second Isaiah) pick up the theme of vindication following suffering, not of vicarious suffering as such.[18] Similarly, the allusion to Deuteronomy 21:22–23 in Acts 5:30 and 10:39 ("hanging him on a tree" [cf. 13:29]) seems to be intended (by Luke) to highlight Jesus's shame and disgrace, and so to serve the same humiliation-vindication motif; to draw the theology of Galatians 3:13 from these Acts references is to read more into the text than sound exegesis allows. And even Acts 20:28 ("the church of the Lord [or of God] that he obtained with his own blood [or with the blood of his own Son]"), not, properly speaking, part of the evangelistic proclamation, remains more than a little puzzling and obscure. In short, *an explicit theology of the death of Jesus is markedly lacking in the proclamation of the Acts sermons.*

Here again we are confronted with a striking variation; for the vicarious sufficiency of the cross is a prominent feature of Paul's gospel,[19] as it is in 1 Peter and Hebrews, not to mention Mark 10:45. Whether this feature of the Acts sermons is a true representation of the primitive gospel or a reflection of Luke's own theology is not entirely clear. The presence of "for our sins" in the gospel handed down to Paul (1 Cor 15:3) and the fact that Luke omits Mark 10:45, or at least prefers a significantly different version of the saying (Luke 22:26), suggest the latter.

17. Acts 2:23, 36; 3:13–15; 4:10; 5:30; 7:52; 10:39; 13:27–28.
18. Acts 3:13, 26; 4:27, 30; so also 8:30–35.
19. Rom 3:25; 1 Cor 15:3; 2 Cor 5:14–21.

MARK 10:45	LUKE 22:26
"The Son of Man came not to be served but to serve, and to give his life a ransom for many."	"The greatest among you must become like the youngest, and the leader like one who serves."

One possible explanation is that Luke was somewhat influenced by the diaspora Judaism of his time that also sought to play down the concept of atonement by sacrifice; the Jerusalem temple had been destroyed, and so the Jewish sacrificial system had been ended. Be that as it may, so far as the gospel preached in the Acts sermons is concerned, we have to say that it lacks a theology of the cross and makes no attempt to attribute a definite atoning significance to the death of Jesus.

Absence of the Tension between Fulfillment and Imminent End

Completely lacking in the sermons of Acts is *the tension between fulfillment and imminent consummation* that was such a prominent feature of Jesus's proclamation of the kingdom[20] and that is equally strong in Paul's message.[21] The parousia, or second coming of Jesus, the nearest equivalent to the coming of the kingdom of God in Jesus's message, is noticeable by its *lack* of prominence. The sense of its imminence barely squeezes through Luke's formulation in Acts 3:20–21, and the day of judgment hardly seems to offer more than a distant threat—certainly not an immediate crisis such as Jesus envisaged.[22] Also lacking is a strong note of realized eschatology, the conviction that the last days are already on us; it is present in Acts 2:15–21 and 3:24, but otherwise wholly absent.

---

20. See, e.g., Matt 13:16–17 // Luke 10:23–24; Matt 12:41–42 // Luke 11:31–32.

21. Marked particularly by the warfare between "flesh" and "Spirit" (Rom 8:1–17; Gal 5:16–17), and in the tug-of-war between "old nature" and "new" (Rom 7:22–25; Eph 4:22–24; Col 3:5–10).

22. Acts 10:42; 17:31; 24:25.

Here the contrast is utterly astonishing. For Jesus proclaimed the presence of the end-time blessings and the imminence of the kingdom as an important part of his message.[23] Likewise, Paul strongly believed that Jesus's resurrection and the gift of the Spirit were the beginning (the firstfruits) of the end-time harvest.[24] And for most of his ministry Paul proclaimed the imminence of the parousia and the end.[25] Particularly worthy of notice is Paul's preservation in 1 Corinthians 16:22 of an Aramaic cry from the earliest church—"Maranatha, Our Lord, come!" It is scarcely possible that the earliest communities of believers in Jerusalem and Palestine lacked this same sense of eschatological fervor and urgency. Indeed, the community of goods, to which Luke refers in Acts 2:44–45 and 4:34–37, is best explained as an expression of this kind of eschatological enthusiasm—property being sold without much thought for the needs of a year hence, the assumption being, presumably, that the Christ would have returned before then. Consequently, the conclusion seems inevitable that Luke has ignored or suppressed this element of the early proclamation and community, presumably because the lapse of time and delay of the parousia made it less appropriate to recall and celebrate.

Limited Role of the Exalted Jesus

Despite what we may presume to be Luke's sense that a long time gap had opened up between the resurrection and the parousia of Jesus, and despite his emphasis on the resurrection of Jesus, there is *hardly any role attributed to the exalted Jesus* in Acts. Of course, the exalted Jesus's bestowal of the Spirit at Pentecost marked the beginning of a new epoch of salvation history (Acts 2:33)—indeed "the last days" (Acts 2:17). And Luke does not hesitate to attribute

---

23. See the full discussion in Dunn, *Jesus Remembered*, vol. 1 of *Christianity in the Making* (Grand Rapids: Eerdmans, 2003), ch. 12.

24. 1 Cor 15:20, 23; Rom 8:23.

25. See especially 1 Thess 1:10; 4:13–18; 1 Cor 7:29–31.

to both Peter and Paul the conviction that Jesus would be judge at the end of days (Acts 10:42; 17:31). Moreover, the exalted Jesus was presumably thought of as the authorization behind those who acted "in the name of Jesus,"[26] and he appears in not a few visions.[27] But there is nothing of the rich sense of union between believer and exalted Lord that, as we shall see, is such a feature of the message of Paul (and of John). He never uses one of Paul's favorite phrases—"in Christ." And the relation between exalted Lord and Holy Spirit, which Paul and John handle so sensitively,[28] is only hinted at in Acts (note Acts 16:6–7). Even more striking, indeed astonishing, is the total absence from Acts of the concept and experience of sonship, which was so central both for Jesus[29] and for Paul, who preserves for us the Aramaic prayer of the early churches, "Abba! Father!," and something of the intensity of their experience of a sonship shared with Christ (Rom 8:15–16; Gal 4:6–7).

God as Subject

Finally under the heading of the proclamation of Jesus in Acts, we should notice the strong "subordinationist" element within the sermons of Acts. Only rarely is Jesus depicted as the *subject* of the action described; everything he does, ministry, resurrection, exaltation, etc., is attributed to God—for example:

Acts 2:22	"Jesus of Nazareth, a man attested to you by God with deeds of power, wonders, and signs that God did through him among you."
Acts 2:32	"This Jesus God raised up, and of that all of us are witnesses."

26. Acts 2:38; 3:6; 4:10, 30; 8:16; 10:48; 16:18; 19:5—and cf. 9:34.

27. Acts 7:55–56; 9:10; 18:9; 22:17–18; 23:11; 26:16, 19.

28. Rom 1:3–4; 8:9–11; 1 Cor 12:3–13; 15:45; John 14:15–16, 26; 16:7–15.

29. See particularly Mark 14:36; Luke 11:2 // Matt 6:9; Matt 11:25–26 // Luke 10:21.

Acts 3:26	"When God raised up his servant, he sent him first to you."
Acts 5:30–31	"The God of our ancestors raised up Jesus. . . . God exalted him at his right hand as Leader and Savior."
Acts 10:38, 40	"God anointed Jesus with the Holy Spirit and with power. . . . God raised him on the third day and allowed him to appear."

The sole reference to the parousia is framed in terms of God *sending* the Christ (Acts 3:20). And in the two references to Jesus as judge it is specifically stated that God appointed him to this office (10:42; 17:31, where Jesus is not even mentioned by name). Moreover, on at least two occasions we should speak more precisely of an "adoptionist" emphasis within the Acts sermons, where the resurrection introduces Jesus to a new status as Son, Messiah, and Lord:

Acts 2:32–36	"This Jesus God raised up . . . being therefore exalted at the right hand of God [Ps 110:1]. . . . Therefore let the entire house of Israel know with certainty that God has made him both Lord and Christ."
Acts 13:32–33	"What God promised to our ancestors he has fulfilled for us, their children, by raising Jesus" (quoting Ps 2:7; Isa 55:3; and Ps 15:10).

This agrees very well with other, probably early forms of Christian preaching (Rom 1:3–4; Heb 5:5), and so very likely reflects the emphasis of the earliest communities. But it contrasts markedly with the cosmic view of Christ that we find particularly in the later Pauline letters and in Revelation.

Other Emphases of Preaching the Good News in Acts

Other emphases distinctive of the Acts portrayal of the preaching of the good news of Jesus are also worth noting.

Call for Repentance and Faith

As in the proclamation of Jesus himself, the good news of the Acts sermons issues in a *call for repentance and faith*. Here the diversity is rather interesting. For, on the one hand, the demand for repentance in Acts is closely parallel to that of Jesus:

Mark 1:15	Mark sums up Jesus's preaching: "The time is fulfilled, and the kingdom of God has come near; repent, and believe in the good news."
Acts 2:38	Peter concludes his Pentecost sermon: "Repent, and be baptized . . . in the name of Jesus Christ."
Acts 3:19	Peter speaks to the people after healing the lame beggar: "Repent therefore, and turn to God so that your sins may be wiped out."
Acts 17:30	Paul concludes his speech to the Areopagus in Athens: "While God has overlooked the times of human ignorance, now he commands all people everywhere to repent."
Acts 26:19–20	Paul's self-defense before King Agrippa: "I was not disobedient to the heavenly vision, but declared . . . also to the Gentiles, that they should repent and turn to God and do deeds consistent with repentance."

So the consistency between Jesus's preaching and that of the apostles in Acts is clear. But somewhat surprisingly, this is in marked contrast to the writings of Paul and John themselves. Paul in fact has little or nothing to say about repentance as such,[30] and John makes no use of the word whatsoever.

In contrast, however, in the call for faith the similarity and dissimilarity run in the opposite direction. Luke regularly refers to the first Christians as "the believers" or "those who have believed,"[31] and this emphasis on faith as the defining characteristic is closely paralleled by both the author of the Gospel of John, who uses the verb "believe" ninety-eight times, and the Pauline letters, which use the verb and noun nearly two hundred times. But the call is specifically for faith *in the Lord Jesus*,[32] and this marks off the gospel in Acts clearly from the gospel of Jesus himself.

One other aspect of Luke's presentation of faith in the earliest communities should perhaps also be mentioned, since it is so distinctive of Acts and sets Acts apart from the rest of the New Testament writings. I refer to the way in which Luke portrays faith in Christ as the effect of miracle without apparently any misgivings on the point,[33] whereas elsewhere in the New Testament this evangelistic, propagandist value of miracle is rather disparaged.[34]

Promise of Forgiveness, Salvation, or the Gift of the Spirit

With the call for repentance and faith is coupled a *promise*—in Acts usually in terms of *forgiveness*,[35] *salvation*,[36] or *the gift of the Spirit*.[37] Here the overlap is rather more extensive with the other proclamations of the New Testament. Jesus's preaching held out the offer of forgiveness and acceptance, and Paul's idea of justifi-

---

30. Rom 2:4; 2 Cor 7:9–10; 12:21.

31. Acts 2:44; 4:32; 5:14; 15:5; 18:27; 19:18; 21:20, 25; 22:19.

32. Acts 9:42; 11:17; 14:23; 16:31.

33. Acts 5:12–14; 9:42; 13:12; 19:17–18.

34. Mark 8:11–12; Matt 12:38–39 // Luke 11:29; John 2:23–25; 4:48; 20:29; 2 Cor 13:3–4.

35. Acts 2:38; 3:19; 5:31; 10:43; 13:38–39; 26:18.

36. Acts 2:21; 4:12; 11:14; 13:26; 16:31.

37. Acts 2:38–39; 3:19; 5:32; cf. 8:15–17; 10:44–47; 19:1–6.

cation is not very far removed from that of forgiveness—though the word "forgiveness" itself occurs only in Ephesians 1:7 and Colossians 1:14 in the Pauline writings, and not at all in the Johannine writings. The idea of salvation (noun or verb) is frequently attributed to Jesus in the first three Gospels,[38] and is regularly used by Paul,[39] though it appears little in the Johannine writings (seven times). With the promise of the Spirit the overlap is different. Jesus spoke very little about the Spirit as such, at least according to the evidence. Only Mark 13:11 could be taken as a promise of the Spirit in times of trial. But the Spirit is very clearly part of the basic gospel message for both Paul and the Johannine circle.[40]

Where again Acts is rather remarkable is in the absence of any ethical corollary to the gospel it portrays. Luke does imply that believers held together in mutual dependence: there are no isolated Christians.[41] But there is little in Acts of moral obligation stemming from the acceptance of the proclamation of Jesus. Most astonishing is the fact that the word "love" (both noun and verb) occurs not at all in Acts, whereas it was integral to the messages of Jesus,[42] of the Pauline epistles (108 instances), and of the Johannine epistles (95 times). Here the contrast is wholly striking.

*   *   *

Can we speak of a single gospel in Acts, a common presentation of Jesus? Can we recognize within the different sermons reproduced by Acts a regular outline that may be said to provide a solid core and that we can call the basic or core proclamation of Jesus by the

38. Mark 3:4; 5:34; 8:35; 10:52; etc.

39. Rom 1:16; 5:9–10; 8:24; 9:27; 10:1, 9–10, 13; etc.

40. See, e.g., Rom 2:29; 8:2, 9, 15; 1 Cor 6:11; 12:13; 2 Cor 1:22; Gal 3:2–3; John 3:5–8; 7:39; 20:22; 1 John 2:27; 3:24.

41. Here is part of the significance of the episodes in Acts 8 and 18:24–19:7.

42. Jesus in fact *reduced* the claim of God to the one word "love." The first and greatest command is "Love God with your whole being and your neighbor as yourself" (Mark 12:28–31); anything that hinders the expression of that love, even the law itself, is to be set aside and ignored (Matt 5:38–48).

earliest church, at least in Luke's presentation of it? The answer is affirmative. The most regular and basic elements are these:

- the proclamation of the resurrection of Jesus
- the call for a response to this proclamation, for repentance and faith in this Jesus
- the promise of forgiveness, salvation, and Spirit to those who so respond.

The presentation of Jesus (the gospel according to Acts) is clear, and its flexibility (the same, yet different) well illustrated.

CHAPTER FIVE

Jesus according to
Paul: Part 1

For Christians generally, Jesus, of course, stands at the center of their faith. And Peter, as Jesus's principal disciple, so strongly commissioned by Jesus himself, according to both Matthew (Matt 16:17–19) and John (John 21:15–17), has always been ranked highly. But for gentile believers the great hero, as the one who did more to bring the gospel to them than any other, is Paul—Saul the persecutor who, encountered by the risen Jesus on the road to Damascus (Acts 9:3–8), became Paul the apostle, the apostle of the gentiles. Those familiar with the Acts account of Christianity's beginnings will readily recall Paul's mission journeys, which dominate the second half of Acts. Mediterranean maps of the time readily set out these journeys, often fascinating students when they study them for the first time.[1] Indeed, so much attention can be given to Paul's missionary journeys as such that the concern Paul devoted to establishing the churches he founded can easily be ignored. It is true that on the first missionary journey (Acts 13–14) Paul did not stay for any great length of time at any place in particular, before returning to his commissioning church in Syrian Antioch (Acts 14:26–28). But it is easy to miss the fact that thereafter Paul's mission focused more on the Aegean, with headquarters first in Corinth (Acts 18:1–18) and then in Ephesus

---

1. See appendix 2 below.

(Acts 19:8–10). And his letters, to Corinth in particular, provide rich and fascinating indications of the challenges he faced and the way he handled them.

One result of this shift of focus from Syria to the Aegean was that Paul became more independent and probably more remote from the Palestinian center of the new movement. This is indicated by two developments in particular. One is that traditional believers in Syria/Palestine became more and more suspicious that Paul was broadening the appeal of the good news of Jesus too widely to gentiles and diminishing what they thought was integral to it, particularly its Jewishness, and particularly the characteristic Jewish requirement of circumcision for all would-be proselytes. Intriguing are the indications, both in Acts and in Paul's own letters, that there were those who thought of Paul's mission as a threat to what they regarded as fundamental to the message of Jesus.[2]

Equally intriguing are the indications that Paul sought to counter these suspicions by making a collection for the poor among the saints in Jerusalem.[3] So determined was he to deliver this probably substantial gift that he set aside the dangers that were evident to him (Rom 15:31), dangers that were all too quickly confirmed when he was mobbed and arrested in Jerusalem (Acts 21:27–36). What happened to the collection that Paul had brought with him? Ironically, Luke never refers explicitly to the gift brought by Paul, alluding to it only in Acts 24:17. We can hardly do other than infer that Luke was embarrassed by the evident failure of Paul's attempt at reconciliation with the Jerusalem leadership. His failure to mention any attempt on the latter's part to defend Paul or to assist him in his imprisonment in Jerusalem is certainly depressingly ominous. Here we see the beginning of the fracture of Jewish Christianity from gentile Christianity that in due course resulted in Jewish Christianity being regarded as a form of early heresy.

---

2. E.g., Acts 15:1, 5; 18:12–13; 2 Cor 10–13; Gal 1:6–9; 3:1–5:26.
3. Rom 15:25–29; 1 Cor 16:1–4; 2 Cor 8–9.

The Distinctiveness of Paul's Gospel

In fact, so much of Paul's gospel is distinctive, but we should at least begin by noting some points that can easily be missed.

Gospel

The good news of Jesus is summed up in the term "gospel." It is too little realized that Christianity owes the term to Paul.[4] The term occurs seventy-six times in the New Testament. And no less than sixty of these are in Paul—for example:

Rom 1:1	"Paul, a servant of Jesus Christ, called to be an apostle, set apart for the gospel of God."
Rom 1:15–16	"Hence my eagerness to proclaim the gospel to you also who are in Rome. For I am not ashamed of the gospel; it is the power of God for salvation to everyone who has faith, to the Jew first and also to the Greek."
Rom 15:19	"From Jerusalem and as far around as Illyricum I have fully proclaimed the gospel of Christ."
1 Cor 4:15	"In Christ Jesus I became your father through the gospel."
1 Cor 9:14	"The Lord commanded that those who proclaim the gospel should get their living by the gospel."
2 Cor 11:4, 7	"If someone comes and proclaims another Jesus than the one we proclaimed, or if you receive . . . a different gospel from the one you accepted. . . ."

---

4. As noted in chapter 2 above.

> Did I commit a sin . . . because I proclaimed the
> gospel of God to you free of charge?"

Gal 1:6–7   "I am astonished that you . . . are turning to a different gospel—not that there is another gospel,
but there are some who . . . want to pervert the
gospel of Christ."

Paul probably derived the term from (Second) Isaiah, where the verbal form, "preach good tidings," is used in passages that evidently greatly influenced both Jesus and his disciples. In Isaiah 40:9, Zion/Jerusalem is urged to renewed confidence as being the "herald of good tidings." Isaiah 52:7 hails the one "who brings good news, who announces salvation, who says to Zion, 'Your God reigns.'" Isaiah 60:6 similarly looks hopefully for those who "shall proclaim the praise of the LORD." And, most famous of all, Isaiah 61:1–2 prophesies: "The Spirit of the Lord GOD is upon me, because the LORD has anointed me; he has sent me to bring good news to the poor . . . to proclaim the year of the LORD's favor."

Luke 4:17–21 indicates that this last passage particularly influenced Jesus, and we can probably see its influence in the first of Jesus's beatitudes (Luke 6:20—"Blessed are you who are poor, for yours is the kingdom of God"). Even more striking is Jesus's reply to the query from John the Baptist as to whether Jesus was indeed the one whose coming the Baptist had announced. Jesus replies that the answer is evident in what he himself is doing—"the blind receive their sight, the lame walk, the lepers are cleansed, the deaf hear, the dead are raised, and [the climax] the poor have the good news brought to them" (Luke 7:22 // Matt 11:5). Paul too was influenced by the same passages, as Romans 10:15 shows most clearly, and, as noted in chapter 2 above, it was Paul who effectively turned the verb "preach good tidings" into the Christian technical term, the noun "gospel," that is, "good tidings." And it is thanks to Paul that we have a good idea of how the first Christians summed up the good news:

> I handed on to you as of first importance what I in turn had
> received: that Christ died for our sins in accordance with

the scriptures, and that he was buried, and that he was raised on the third day in accordance with the scriptures, and that he appeared to Cephas, then to the twelve. Then he appeared to more than five hundred brothers at one time. . . . Then he appeared to James, then to all the apostles. Last of all, as to one untimely born, he appeared also to me. (1 Cor 15:3–8)

Here, of course, we are not talking about the distinctiveness of Paul's gospel. What is distinctive is the care he takes to make it clear that his gospel was *not* distinctive: it was the gospel that he had received when he was converted. The distinctiveness is that Paul had to make this claim and no doubt in effect repeat it often. For he had not been a disciple of Jesus. And his previous role as a persecutor of the first believers would have been well known. As he observes in his letter to the Galatians, when he began to take the gospel farther into Syria and Cilicia, he was still largely unknown to the churches of Judea. All they heard was that "the one who formerly was persecuting us is now proclaiming the faith he once tried to destroy" (Gal 1:23).

Paul and the Life and Ministry of Jesus

As we shall see, the really distinctive feature of Paul's gospel was the degree to which it focused on Jesus's death and resurrection. But first we need to note what appears to be an equally distinctive corollary: that *Paul seems to show little interest in Jesus's life and ministry prior to his death and resurrection.* Indeed, if we were dependent solely on Paul's letters for our knowledge of the ministry of Jesus, we would know very little. He certainly knew that Jesus was a Jew, "born of a woman, born under the law" (Gal 4:4); indeed, that he "was descended from David according to the flesh" (Rom 1:3–4). He knew that Jesus had brothers (1 Cor 9:5; Gal 1:19). And, of course, he recalls Jesus's institution of the Lord's Supper (1 Cor 11:23–26). But beyond that we have only allusions, to Christ's "meekness and gentleness" (2 Cor 10:1), to his "compassion" (Phil 1:8), and to the fact that "Christ did not please himself" (Rom 15:3).

So it is not unjustified, and for us hardly irrelevant, to ask whether Paul had much knowledge of and indeed much interest in the life and ministry of Jesus prior to his death and resurrection. And in fact, rather embarrassingly, the evidence is rather limited. The embarrassment is somewhat ameliorated since, as we shall see, it is quite possible to deduce that Paul was deeply influenced by *Jesus's teaching*. It is surprisingly true, nevertheless, that only three specific traditions are attributed explicitly to Jesus—all indeed in one letter:

1 Cor 7:10–11	Paul cites the Lord's command regarding divorce (cf. Mark 10:11 parr.).
1 Cor 9:14	"The Lord commanded that those who proclaim the gospel should get their living by the gospel" (cf. Matt 10:10 // Luke 10:7).
1 Cor 11:23–25	The institution of the Lord's Supper, introduced rather strikingly: "I received from the Lord what I also handed on to you."

There are, however, a number of allusions to or echoes of Jesus's teaching in Paul's paraenesis that are widely recognized. The most striking include the following (esp. the words in italics):[5]

Rom 12:14	*"Bless those who persecute you; bless* and do not curse them."
Luke 6:27–28	"Love your enemies . . . *bless* those who *curse* you."
Matt 5:44	"Love your enemies and pray for *those who persecute you.*"

5. See also Rom 12:17 and 1 Thess 5:15 (Matt 5:38–48 // Luke 6:27–36); Rom 13:7 (Mark 12:17 parr.); Rom 14:13 (Mark 9:42 parr.).

Rom 14:14	"I know and am persuaded in the Lord Jesus that nothing is unclean in itself."
Mark 7:15	"There is nothing outside a person that . . . can defile."
1 Cor 13:2	"If [you] have all *faith*, so as to *remove mountains*."
Matt 17:20	"If you *have faith* . . . you will say to this *mountain*, '*Move* from here to there,' and it will *move*."
1 Thess 5:2, 4	"You yourselves know very well that the day of the Lord will come like a thief in the night. . . . But you, beloved, are not in darkness, for that day to surprise you like a thief."
Matt 24:43	"Understand this: if the owner of the house had known in what part of the night the thief was coming, he would have stayed awake."
1 Thess 5:13	"Be at peace among yourselves."
Mark 9:50	"Be at peace with one another."

Otherwise, nonetheless, we learn little of Jesus's life and ministry from Paul's letters. Indeed, had we only Paul's letters, we would know next to nothing about Jesus's ministry and teaching, apart from his death and resurrection. Does this mean that Paul had no real interest in Jesus's ministry and was in effect interested only in its climax? That is hardly likely. These strong echoes of Jesus's teaching surely imply that one of Paul's self-appointed tasks when he set up a new church was to pass on a substantial amount of Jesus tradition—Jesus's teaching to which he could refer, as just illustrated, when the occasion demanded. This is confirmed by Paul's references to the "traditions" that he passed on to the churches he founded,[6]

6. 1 Cor 11:2, 23; 15:3; 2 Thess 2:15; 3:6.

which presumably included basic information about Jesus's life and ministry for those to whom Jesus was an entirely unknown figure. And probably also he passed on a considerable synopsis of Jesus's teaching, to which he could refer, as in the examples just cited.

In addition, we can be confident that when, for example, Paul said, "I know and am persuaded in the Lord Jesus that nothing is unclean in itself" (Rom 14:14), he was well aware of the Jesus tradition, probably in the form known to us from Mark 7:14–23. Or again, it is very hard to read of Paul's conflict with his fellow Jewish believers, as to whether it should be acceptable to eat with (gentile) "sinners" (Gal 2:11–17), without recalling Jesus's similar conflicts with Pharisees regarding his readiness to "eat with sinners" (Mark 2:15–17 parr.). And it surely is almost impossible to believe that when Paul cited the "Abba! Father!" prayer, as evidence of the Spirit of the Son sent into their hearts (Gal 4:6–7; Rom 8:15–17), he was unaware that this form of prayer was distinctive of Jesus's own prayers and that it was Jesus who began the tradition of so praying. It is highly probable, in fact, that such passages and the allusions to Jesus's teaching refer to and reflect the foundational teaching that Paul set out when he established a new congregation.

Finally we should note the element of *imitatio Christi* that appears in some of Paul's exhortation. So in particular, Romans 13:14: "put on the Lord Jesus Christ." Similarly later in the same letter: we ought "not to please ourselves . . . for Christ too did not please himself" (Rom 15:1–5). To be sure, the reference is primarily to Christ's passion (Rom 15:3). But in a context of community fellowship (Rom 14:1–15:6), where it is *"the Christ"* who is referred to (Rom 15:3), and with an echo of his being "a servant of the circumcised" (Rom 15:8), it is unlikely that many would think solely of Jesus's death. Such an appeal to Jesus as an antidote to communal disaffection is also explicit in 1 Corinthians 11:1 ("Be imitators of me, as I am of Christ") and in Philippians 2:5 ("Let the same mind be in you that was in Christ Jesus"). It is hardly straining either evidence or probabilities to infer that Paul's readers would give content to such exhortations by recalling stories about and teaching of Jesus.

Similarly we should recall that Paul refers to Jesus as "a pattern of teaching" (Rom 6:17—"the one to whom you were handed over as a pattern of teaching"). This suggests an ethical corollary of baptism understood as a commitment to a way of living modeled on Jesus's teaching. A near parallel would be Colossians 2:6: "as you received the tradition of Christ Jesus as Lord, walk in him." This can hardly be understood other than as an exhortation to Christian conduct modeled on the traditions of Jesus passed on to new converts. Paul's urging that those who receive his letter should behave "in accordance with Christ Jesus" (Rom 15:5) has a similar implication.

We may infer, then, that when Mark broadened out the meaning of "gospel" to include the ministry of Jesus prior to his death and resurrection, he was simply making explicit what had been implicit in the message that Paul passed on to his churches when he established them. The good news included the recollection of the character of Jesus's ministry and the content of his teaching, climaxing in his death and resurrection. The distinctiveness of Paul's gospel was not that it was different from the gospel preached by other first Christians. The distinctiveness was his conviction that the gospel was also for gentiles.

How then did Paul fill out his understanding of the gospel with its centrality on the death and resurrection of Christ?

That Christ Died for Our Sins and Was Raised on the Third Day

As we have seen above, this is how Paul summarized the gospel that had been passed on to him (1 Cor 15:3).

Atoning Death of Jesus

Certainly *the atoning death of Jesus* was at the heart of the gospel for Paul:

Rom 3:24–25   "They are now justified by his grace as a gift, through the redemption that is in Christ Jesus, whom God put forward as a sacrifice of atonement by his blood, effective through faith."

Rom 5:6, 8 "At the right time Christ died for the ungodly. . . . God proves his love for us in that while we still were sinners Christ died for us."

Rom 8:3 "By sending his own Son in the likeness of sinful flesh, and to deal with sin, he condemned sin in the flesh."

1 Cor 5:7 "Our paschal lamb, Christ, has been sacrificed."

2 Cor 5:15 "He died for all, so that those who live might live no longer for themselves, but for him who died and was raised for them."

Gal 3:13 "Christ redeemed us from the curse of the law by becoming a curse for us—for it is written, 'Cursed is everyone who hangs on a tree'" (Deut 21:23).

Behind this lies the theology of sacrifice in ancient Judaism, made most explicit in the Day of Atonement ritual described in Leviticus 16. The key point in the ritual was when the high priest laid his hands on one of the two goats presented before him, and thereby put the sins just confessed "on the head of the goat" (Lev 16:21). The goat was then sent into the wilderness, carrying the sins of the people away. The clear implication was that those who had committed these sins were now free from them. There had been an *interchange*: the burden of sin transferred to the sinless one, leaving the one who had committed the sin free of it and its consequences. That seems to be the theological rationale of Israel's sacrifice of atonement, which Paul (and the first Christians) took over in regarding the death of Jesus as just such a sacrifice. The point is clearest in 2 Corinthians 5:21: "He who knew no sin, God made sin for our sake." For Paul, however, Jesus's death was not just such a sacrifice, but was, in effect, *the* sacrifice to which Israel's sacrificial system pointed forward—a claim that, as we shall see, the writer of Hebrews made the center of his theology.

The centrality of the death of Christ in Paul's theology is further indicated by his use of the phrase "in/through his blood."[7] This cannot adequately be understood except as a reference to Christ's death as a sacrifice, since it was precisely the manipulation of the victim's blood which was the decisive act of atonement.[8] Likewise Paul's talk of Jesus's death as "for sins,"[9] or "for us."[10] Galatians 3:13 has one of Paul's most striking claims: that "Christ redeemed us from the curse of the law by becoming a curse for us—for it is written, 'Cursed is everyone who hangs on a tree'" (Deut 21:23). And he also uses the powerful imagery of "redemption" and "reconciliation," as again in Romans 3:24 and powerfully in 2 Corinthians 5:18–20.

Jesus Raised from the Dead

Equally fundamental for Paul was the central Christian belief that God had *raised Jesus from the dead*. The point could hardly be clearer than when, as we have seen, Paul summarizes the foundational Christian belief: "That he was raised on the third day in accordance with the scriptures," as confirmed by the succession of witnesses that he goes on to cite (1 Cor 15:3–8). Indeed, the whole of 1 Corinthians 15 shows just how fundamental the resurrection of Jesus was for Paul's gospel. Those long familiar with the passage probably find it hard to appreciate what a huge impact it must have made when first read and listened to. But the fact that Paul takes such pains to bring home the central importance of that part of his message surely puts the point beyond dispute. And Paul does not hesitate to underline the point: "If Christ has

7. Rom 3:25; 5:9; Eph 1:7; 2:13; Col 1:20.
8. Lev 4:5–7, 16–18, 25, 30, 34; 16:14–19.
9. Rom 4:25; 8:3; 1 Cor 15:3; Gal 1:4.
10. Rom 5:6–8; 8:32; 2 Cor 5:14–15, 21; Gal 2:20; 3:13; 1 Thess 5:9–10; also Eph 5:2, 25.

not been raised, then our proclamation has been in vain and your faith has been in vain" (1 Cor 15:14); "if Christ has not been raised, your faith is futile and you are still in your sins" (1 Cor 15:17). He can even speak of Jesus's resurrection as fully equivalent to the creation of humanity. Jesus is "the last Adam" (1 Cor 15:45)—his resurrection, as beginning a whole new life, beyond death, unique in the same way that Adam's creation was unique.

> Christ has been raised from the dead, the first fruits of those who have died. For since death came through a human being, the resurrection of the dead has also come through a human being; for as all die in Adam, so all will be made alive in Christ. (1 Cor 15:20–22)

So it is hardly surprising that elsewhere Paul underlines the importance of Jesus's resurrection. Very striking is the opening paragraph in his letter to Rome when he summarizes his gospel—"the gospel concerning [God's] Son, who was descended from David according to the flesh and was declared to be the Son of God with power according to the Spirit of holiness by resurrection from the dead, Jesus Christ our Lord" (Rom 1:3–4). Typical of Paul is the conclusion to his exposition of Abraham's justification: what had been "reckoned" to Abraham (righteousness—Gen 15:6) "will be reckoned to us who believe in him who raised Jesus our Lord from the dead" (Rom 4:24).

According to these passages, the resurrection of Jesus also indicated his status as "Lord." As Paul puts it later in the same letter: "to this end Christ died and lived again, so that he might be Lord of both the dead and the living" (Rom 14:9). Most striking is the climax of Philippians 2:6–11, usually regarded as a pre-Pauline hymn quoted by Paul:

> Therefore God also highly exalted him and gave him the name that is above every name, so that at the name of Jesus every knee should bend . . . and every tongue should confess that Jesus Christ is Lord, to the glory of God the Father.

Not least striking is Paul's use of Psalm 110:1 to express the conviction that Jesus, having been raised from the dead, was now God's vice-regent: "The LORD says to my lord, 'Sit at my right hand until I make your enemies your footstool.'"[11] In fact, Paul's usual way of referring to Christ is as "the Lord Jesus Christ," or simply as "the Lord."[12] The central significance of the resurrection for Paul's gospel could hardly be clearer.

With Christ

What was of fundamental importance for Paul was that believers could not simply affirm these foundational beliefs but could *identify with them* in a way and degree hitherto unknown. This is most clearly indicated by Paul's remarkable use of compounds that include "with" across his letters[13]—for example, "groan together with" (Rom 8:22), "reign with" (1 Cor 4:8), "suffer with" (1 Cor 12:26), "die with" and "live with" (2 Cor 7:3), and "participate with" (Phil 4:14). Most significantly, however, he uses such compound verbs to describe an actual sharing in Christ's death and life: for example, "suffer with" (Rom 8:17), "crucified with" (Gal 2:19), "buried with" (Col 2:12), "raised with" (Col 3:1), "live with" (Rom 6:8), and "glorified with" (Rom 8:17). Since "in Christ" is such a prominent feature of Paul's writings, the frequency with which he uses "with Christ" to express the same sense of a shared dependence on a common experience of participation in Christ is often missed. The centrality of the theme to Paul's gospel is nowhere more clearly expressed than in two passages from his letter to Rome:

Rom 6:4–8   "So then we were *buried with* him through baptism into death. . . . For if we have become *knit*

---

11. Rom 8:34; 1 Cor 15:25; Eph 1:20; Col 3:1.

12. In Paul's letters, "Lord Jesus Christ" (in varying order) occurs nearly 70 times; "the Lord," more than 140 times.

13. More than half of the forty occurrences appear only in Paul in the NT.

together with the very likeness of his death, we shall certainly also be *knit together with* the very likeness of his resurrection. Knowing this, that our old nature has been *crucified with* him. . . . But if we have *died with* Christ, we believe that we shall also *live with* him."

Rom 8:16–17 "The Spirit *bears witness with* our spirit that we are children of God. And if children, also heirs— heirs of God and *heirs together with* Christ, provided that we *suffer with* him in order that we might also be *glorified with* him."[14]

So it was not simply the belief in Jesus's death and resurrection that was central to Paul's gospel; it was also the sense that those who responded to the gospel could realistically share in what was thus proclaimed, could already experience both a dying of and a dying to their old self-centered nature, and a new life welling up within and giving a new goal and motivation to all they did.

Justification through Faith in Jesus

One of the striking features of Paul's theology (and gospel) is the range of metaphors he draws on.

Metaphors of Sacrifice

In a tradition where animal sacrifice was the characteristic way of ensuring positive relations with the cult god, it is natural that the metaphor of sacrifice was so powerful in the earliest Christians' attempts to make sense of Jesus's death. But Paul also used many *different metaphors* for the salvation that his gospel offered and

14. See also Col 2:12–13; Eph 2:5–6; 2 Tim 2:11–12.

promised. One was "redemption"—the imagery taken from the buying back of a slave or war captive, and echoing Israel's deliverance from Egypt. So, for example:

Rom 3:24   "They are now justified by his grace as a gift, through the redemption that is in Christ Jesus."

1 Cor 1:30 "Christ Jesus ... became for us wisdom from God, and righteousness and sanctification and redemption."

Col 1:14   "In whom we have redemption, the forgiveness of sins."

Similarly with "liberation" or "freedom." For example:

Rom 6:18   "You, having been set free from sin, have become slaves of righteousness."

Rom 8:2   "The law of the Spirit of life in Christ Jesus has set you free from the law of sin and of death."

Gal 2:4   "The freedom we have in Christ Jesus."

Gal 5:1   "For freedom Christ has set us free. Stand firm, therefore, and do not submit again to a yoke of slavery."

And again with the imagery of "reconciliation"— the bringing together of two parties at enmity with each other into a new peace and cooperation. Note particularly the following:

Rom 5:10   "If while we were enemies, we were reconciled to God through the death of his Son, much more surely, having been reconciled, will we be saved by his life."

2 Cor 5:18-19   "All this is from God, who reconciled us to himself through Christ, and has given us the ministry of reconciliation; that is, in Christ God was reconciling the world to himself, not counting their trespasses against them, and entrusting the message of reconciliation to us."

It is important to appreciate the metaphorical character of these images. They are not literal and do not fit easily together. There is indeed a danger of making one or another the key and trying to fit the others into it. This has sometimes happened with the particularly Johannine metaphor of being "born again or from above" (notably John 3:3-8). But as with metaphors generally, they are images and not literal, illustrating an aspect, particularly an experiential aspect of conversion to Christ.

Metaphors from the Law Court

Historically it was metaphors from the law court in which *the accused person was accounted not guilty or justified* that were most important for Paul. The rediscovery of this theme became a key feature of the European Reformation. Its importance for Paul is easily illustrated. For example, in Romans he sums up his indictment of humankind by quoting Psalm 143:2: "For 'no human being will be will be justified in his sight' by deeds prescribed by the law, for through the law comes knowledge of sin" (Rom 3:20). And then he goes on in one of the most crucial passages of his writings to spell out how his gospel sees acceptance or justification by God to be accomplished:

> All have sinned and fall short of the glory of God; they are now justified by his grace as a gift, through the redemption that is in Christ Jesus, whom God put forward as a sacrifice of atonement by his blood, effective through faith. He did this to show his righteousness, because in his divine forbearance he had passed over the sins previously com-

mitted; it was to prove at the present time that he himself is righteous and that he justifies the one who has faith in Jesus. (Rom 3:23–26)

And Paul later recalls the key point when he gives his own testimony in Philippians 3:8–9:

> I regard everything as loss because of the surpassing value of knowing Christ Jesus my Lord. For his sake I have suffered the loss of all things, and I regard them as rubbish, in order that I may gain Christ and be found in him, not having a righteousness of my own that comes from the law, but one that comes through faith in Christ.

As indicated, the image of justification or acquittal is drawn from the law court. The conviction is that God accepts the sinner who trusts in him, who throws himself/herself on God's mercy, even though he/she is guilty of acting against God. "Righteousness" in Hebrew thought denoted fulfilling the obligations that arise out of a relationship; the person who fulfills such obligations is deemed righteous.[15] The basic Jewish logic or theology was that God, having created the world, had taken upon himself the obligation to sustain it. And having chosen Israel to be his people, God had accepted the further obligation to look after Israel, to be faithful even when Israel was unfaithful. So, for Israel God's righteousness was not essentially punitive but saving. This is why the term "righteousness" in the Old Testament is sometimes better translated as "salvation," or "vindication."[16] This is the root of Paul's gospel, as Martin Luther realized when he read Romans 1:16–17 with fresh eyes: "I am not ashamed of the gospel; it is the power of God for salvation to everyone who has faith. . . . For in it the righteousness of God is revealed through faith for faith; as it is written: 'The one who is righteous will live by faith'" (Hab 2:4).

---

15. As most strikingly in 1 Sam 24:17. Similarly Judah's verdict on his relationship with Tamar (Gen 38:26).

16. So in NRSV translation of Isa 62:2 and Mic 6:5; 7:9.

In other words, God's acceptance was not dependent on proving our worthiness ("You are worth it"), but dependent solely on God's grace. Abraham himself was the determinative precedent, as Paul went on to argue in Romans 4; and Israel's election, of the "no-people" Israel as God's people (Rom 9:25-26), proved the same point.

Faith and Works of the Law

The key point for Paul was that justification, God's accounting sinners acceptable despite their sin, was by *faith* and was not determined by the individual's doing the law, or by *"works of the law."* This evidently came home to Paul through his own experience (the justified persecutor), and especially through the success of his gentile mission. Gentiles had received the Spirit/grace of God without reference to the law. As Paul asks his Galatian converts: "The only thing I want to learn from you is this: Did you receive the Spirit by doing the works of the law or by believing what you heard?" (Gal 3:2). Evidently Paul was confronted with the fact that others (Jewish Christian missionaries, we assume) had come to his Galatian converts and had insisted that the latter could not be counted members of the people of Israel's God unless they were first circumcised and observed the Jewish laws of clean and unclean foods. In response Paul insisted forcibly that justification was by faith, and by faith alone. This was the argument he had won in Jerusalem, when the earliest Christian council, chaired, it would appear, by James, the brother of Jesus (Acts 15:13-22), agreed that gentile converts need not be circumcised (Gal 2:1-10). That agreement, however, had been put in question in the Christian grouping in Antioch, when "certain people came from James" and insisted that the Jewish food laws should be maintained in the new Christian fellowship groups. They had been so persuasive that all the other Jewish believers, including Paul's close colleague Barnabas (you can almost hear the sob in Paul's writing when he recalls the incident), had separated in fellowship meals from the gentile believers (Gal 2:11-14). Hence,

Paul's condemnation of what he had no hesitation in designating as "hypocrisy" and "inconsistent with the truth of the gospel," and his indignant response:

> We ourselves are Jews by birth and not Gentile sinners; yet we know that a person is justified not by the works of the law but through *faith in Jesus Christ*. And we have come to *believe in Christ Jesus*, so that we might be justified by *faith in Christ*, and not by doing works of the law. (Gal 2:15–16)

Paul's point is clear. If we bring it up to date, we might note the equivalent danger of adding something to the basic summons to faith in Christ as though that something was equally important as faith—whether episcopacy, an infallible papacy, believer's baptism, or biblical inerrancy. Paul's point would surely be the same: to make such additions fundamental to Christianity still subverts the gospel. It is little wonder that some translators reinforced Paul's point by adding "alone" to what Paul wrote in Galatians 2:15–16: "not by the works of the law but through faith in Jesus Christ, faith alone."

Unfortunately, in the Protestant theology of justification that followed from the Reformation, Paul's point was somewhat misdirected, Paul's warning against making justification depend on "works of the law" being taken as a warning not to trust in "good works." To broaden out Paul's point as a warning not to trust in good works is one thing. But if the consequence is that we miss Paul's actual point here, that is hardly acceptable. As Galatians 2:11–16 makes clear, what Paul was objecting to was the attempt in effect to make justification (of gentiles) conditional on their doing "works of the law," that is, on the requirement that gentiles should "judaize," that is, become or at least live like Jews. As Paul asked Peter in frustrated indignation: "If you, though a Jew, live like a Gentile and not like a Jew, how can you compel the Gentiles [gentile believers] to live like Jews?" (Gal 2:14).

This is the point that has often been misunderstood: Paul was not abandoning the law or making a total break with the law. As he says, for example, in 1 Corinthians 7:19: "Circumcision is nothing, and uncircumcision is nothing; but obeying the commandments of God is everything." Or, as he points out in Romans 8:3–4: when God sent his Son, "he condemned sin in the flesh, so that the just requirement of the law might be fulfilled in us, who walk not according to the flesh but according to the Spirit." Or, as he noted earlier in the same letter: since God justifies both circumcised and uncircumcised in the same way, by the same faith, "Do we then overthrow the law by this faith? By no means! On the contrary, we uphold the law" (Rom 3:30–31). The point, once again, and worth repeating, is that Paul was not reacting against the law as such or good works as such. He was reacting against the assumption that gentile believers must be circumcised and must observe Israel's food laws. Which is to say, he was reacting against the assumption that the gospel was exclusively for Jews and that the gospel therefore required gentiles in effect to become Jews, by being circumcised and observing the Jewish food laws. It still does not mean that for Paul justification was by anything more than or by anything other than faith. But faith still needed the law, apart from its specifically Israel rulings, to guide life. Or, as Paul put it later in his letter to the Galatians: "In Christ Jesus neither circumcision nor uncircumcision counts for anything; the only thing that counts is faith working through love" (Gal 5:6).

* * *

Justification through faith in Jesus is so central, both to Paul's own understanding, exposition, and living out of faith and in the history of Western Christianity, that it is well to pause at this point and reflect on it and on all that it involves and implies for Christianity, today as in crucial turning points of the past. So we break our study of Paul's understanding of the good news of Jesus at this point.

CHAPTER SIX

Jesus according to
Paul: Part 2

The importance of Paul's understanding and teaching on the theme of justification by faith (alone) was so central and decisive—both in the beginnings of gentile Christianity and in the recalling of sixteenth-century Europe "back to the Bible"—that it is easy to miss or ignore how much richer and fuller was Paul's recollection of what Jesus had done and the extent to which Jesus was at the center of his whole life and mission. Since the Pauline letters make up such an important part of the New Testament, it is well worth spending another chapter to explore the gospel according to Paul more fully.

Participation in Christ

In Christ/In the Lord

Here is another element in Paul's theology and understanding of the gospel and its outworking that can be too easily neglected. In fact, Paul uses the phrase "in Christ" some eighty-three times in his letters, and "in the Lord" forty-seven times.[1] This too is a dis-

---

1. We could add "in him // whom." These phrases, for example, appear consistently (twelve times) in Col 1:14–19 and 2:3–15.

tinctively Pauline feature. Elsewhere in the New Testament, outside the Pauline corpus, the phrase occurs only in 1 Peter, which, somewhat surprisingly, is the most Pauline of the non-Pauline letters.[2] It also should not be ignored that Paul uses these phrases far more than any of the metaphors that we naturally draw from his writings. This in turn presumably signifies that these phrases were at the heart of his understanding and outliving of the gospel that he proclaimed. Some examples:

Rom 3:22–24	"There is no distinction, since all have sinned and fall short of the glory of God; they are now justified by his grace as a gift, through the redemption that is in Christ Jesus."
Rom 6:11	"So you also must consider yourselves dead to sin and alive to God in Christ Jesus."
Rom 6:23	"The wages of sin is death, but the free gift of God is eternal life in Christ Jesus our Lord."
Rom 8:1–2	"There is therefore now no condemnation for those who are in Christ Jesus. For the law of the Spirit of life in Christ Jesus has set you free from the law of sin and of death."
1 Cor 1:4	"The grace of God that has been given you in Christ Jesus."
1 Cor 15:22	"So all will be made alive in Christ."
2 Cor 5:19	"In Christ God was reconciling the world."
Gal 3:14	"In order that in Christ Jesus the blessing of Abraham might come to the Gentiles."

2. 1 Pet 3:16; 5:10, 14.

Gal 5:6   "In Christ Jesus neither circumcision nor uncir-
              cumcision counts for anything."

Phil 4:19   "My God will fully satisfy every need of yours ac-
              cording to his riches in glory in Christ Jesus."

1 Thess 5:18 "Give thanks in all circumstances; for this is the
              will of God in Christ Jesus for you."

Similarly, Paul regularly sends greetings to individuals "in the
Lord" (e.g., Rom 16:8–13):

1 Cor 4:17   Timothy is his "beloved and faithful child in the
              Lord."

1 Cor 9:1   He calls the Corinthians his workmanship "in the
              Lord."

Philem 16   Onesimus is a beloved brother "both in the flesh
              and in the Lord."

Paul's gospel can indeed be summed up in just these terms:
(1) God has acted redemptively "in Christ"; (2) saving grace has
been experienced by believers "in Christ"; (3) believers now
live life "in the Lord." "In Christ" indicates a bound-upness with
Christ, a oneness with Christ. Paul's perception of his whole life
as a Christ-believer—its source, its identity, and its responsibilities—could be summed up in these phrases. It is important to
note that this was not just a matter of belief for Paul. There was
undoubtedly an experiential dimension, an experience of being
caught up with the risen and living Christ. Paul evidently felt
himself (an emotional dimension can hardly be ignored) to be
caught up "in Christ," to be doing what he did "with Christ," sus-
tained and borne along by Christ. We see here an evident sense
of Christ's living presence as a more or less constant factor, from
which Paul consciously and subconsciously drew inspiration and
strength for all his activities.

It is interesting to note that Paul can put the imagery in reverse order—not just believers "in Christ," but "Christ in us." Note, for example:

Gal 2:20	"It is no longer I who live, but it is Christ who lives in me."
Rom 8:10	"If Christ is in you, though the body is dead because of sin, the Spirit is life because of righteousness."
2 Cor 13:5	"Do you not realize that Jesus Christ is in you?"
Col 1:27	". . . how great among the Gentiles are the riches of the glory of this mystery, which is Christ in you, the hope of glory."

The sense of total engagement with Christ, of Christ as the life force working in him and through him, could hardly be clearer.

Into Christ

Not surprisingly, Paul also speaks on several occasions of individuals brought "into Christ." The most notable example is his talk of converts "having been baptized into Christ." For example:

Rom 6:3	"Do you not know that all of us who have been baptized into Christ Jesus were baptized into his death?"
Gal 3:27	"As many of you as were baptized into Christ have clothed yourselves with Christ."

It is difficult to avoid the basic sense of "into," implying movement into a location, a movement of incorporation. So in Romans 6:3, the implication is of becoming a participant in Christ, as in Romans 5:12–17 the individual was already a participant in the humanity of Adam. And the imagery in Galatians 3:27 is correlated with the accompanying metaphor of "clothing with/ putting on Christ." To be "baptized into Christ" is to be absorbed into the persona of Christ. It is hard to escape the implication of some sort of identification with or a sense of bound-upness with Christ.

Again, not surprising in view of this common usage, and indicating what Paul took to be a basic given of his life as a Christ-believer, is his imagery of the Christian community as *the body of Christ*. The thought is not yet of the wide range of believers as the (universal) body of Christ (even if only those of whom Paul was particularly thinking, in Asia Minor and Greece), but of believers gathered in a particular place like Corinth as the body of Christ in that place—those "in Christ" bound together as embodying Christ's presence in Corinth. This is presumably what Paul was thinking of when he wrote 1 Corinthians 12:13, speaking of the Corinthian believers as "all baptized into one body," in Corinth. The thought is of those referred to as becoming members of the body of Christ (1 Cor 12:14–27). That passage underlines the privilege and responsibility of those who were members of that body. Each member of the body had by definition his/her particular function or "gift," as Paul puts it. The body could function properly only when each member fulfilled his/her particular function, only when each exercised the gift given to each and for which he/ she was responsible (1 Cor 12:8–11). "To each is given the manifestation of the Spirit for the common good" (1 Cor 12:7). In Paul's thinking, the Christian community (the body) could only be "built up"—a common metaphor in chapter 14 (vv. 3, 5, 12, 26)—when each of the members of the body exercised the gift(s) given to each, or perhaps more precisely, given *through* each.

We will return to what was obviously a major theme for Paul below. But here we should at least note in passing that Paul had no conception of an order of priesthood. There were no priests, no one functioning as "priest" in his churches (or indeed in any New Testament churches). He used the image of priestly ministry as a general way of referring to the service of the gospel (as in Phil 2:25), but also as a way of characterizing everyday discipleship, the responsibility of all believers (Rom 12:1).

Like Christ

It is worth noting that Paul saw this relationship to Christ as a developing one—what came to be categorized as "sanctification." The goal of salvation was to *become like Christ*:

Rom 8:29   "Conformed to the image of [God's] Son, in order that he might be the firstborn within a large family."

2 Cor 3:18   "Being transformed into the same image from one degree of glory to another."

Col 3:10   "Being renewed in knowledge according to the image of its creator."

So, being a member of the body of Christ was neither a static nor a final condition. In the letters to the Colossians and the Ephesians Paul includes the idea of growing up "in every way into him who is the head, into Christ," so that each part working properly "promotes the body's growth in building itself up in love" (Eph 4:15–16; similarly Col 2:19).

A final thought not to be missed is that such growth included becoming like Christ in his death. Baptism was baptism "into his death" (Rom 6:3). As it was necessary for Christ to die, in order that by his resurrection he might introduce a life beyond death, so there had to be a sharing in Christ's death in order to experience also his life beyond death, a life that lasts through the death of this body. For example:

Rom 6:5   "If we have been united with him in a death like
           his, we will certainly be united with him in a res-
           urrection like his."

Rom 8:17   "If children, then heirs, heirs of God and joint
           heirs with Christ—if in fact, we suffer with him
           so that we may also be glorified with him."

Or as Paul expressed his hope and ambition in what was probably
one of his last letters:

Phil 3:10–11   "I want to know Christ and the power of his res-
               urrection and the sharing of his sufferings by be-
               coming like him in his death, if somehow I may
               attain the resurrection from the dead."

The Gift of the Spirit

The Gift of the Spirit as the Defining Mark

This again is a rather neglected feature of Paul's understanding
of the Christian faith. The debate occasioned by the rise of Pen-
tecostalism, where classically Spirit-baptism was seen as distinct
from and subsequent to conversion or the beginning of the individual's life as a Christian, rather confused the point. But *the
gift of the Spirit as the decisive mark of the Christian* was crucial
for Paul.

Consider, for example, Paul's rejoinder to those of his Galatian converts who were being persuaded that to be Christian they
needed to "do the works of the law" by being circumcised:

The only thing I want to learn from you is this: Did you
receive the Spirit by doing the works of the law or by believing what you heard? Are you so foolish? Having started
with the Spirit, are you now ending with the flesh? . . .
Does God supply you with the Spirit and work miracles

among you by your doing the works of the law, or by your believing what you heard? (Gal 3:2-5)

And his exposition of how Abraham was justified by faith climaxes with the striking claim: "Christ redeemed us from the curse of the law by becoming a curse for us . . . in order that in Christ Jesus the blessing of Abraham might come to the Gentiles, so that we might receive the promise of the Spirit through faith" (Gal 3:13-14). Similarly he reminds his Thessalonian converts that "in spite of persecution you received the word with joy inspired by the Holy Spirit" (1 Thess 1:6). And in a powerful passage in a letter to the Corinthians he commends the recipients of his letter: "You show that you are a letter of Christ, prepared by us, written not with ink but with the Spirit of the living God, not on tablets of stone [like the Ten Commandments] but on tablets of human hearts. . . . [God] has made us competent to be ministers of a new covenant, not of letter but of spirit; for the letter kills, but the Spirit gives life" (2 Cor 3:3, 6). It is clear from such passages that it was the gift of the Spirit that Paul saw as marking out those who had responded positively to his message.

What is often missed, however, is the fact that Paul regarded the gift of the Spirit as the defining or determinative mark of a believer in Christ. Of course, he understood relationship to the risen Christ as fundamental to being a believer. He saw baptism in the name of Christ as the initiation of the Christian life. But the nearest he comes to providing a definition of a believer in Christ is in terms of that person having received the Spirit. As he says in his great "Spirit chapter" in the letter to Rome: "Anyone who does not have the Spirit of Christ does not belong to him" (Rom 8:9). Or, as he puts it in more positive terms a few verses later: "All who are led by the Spirit of God are children of God" (Rom 8:14). It was their reception of the Spirit that for Paul made believers members of Christ, of Christ's body. He takes up the Baptist's imagery of the coming one baptizing in the Spirit as the counterpart and completion of his (the Baptist's) own baptism in water (Mark 1:8 parr.): "In the one Spirit we were all baptized into one body . . . and we were all made to drink of one Spirit" (1 Cor 12:13). Or consider the somewhat complex application Paul makes of Moses, coming out from an encounter with the Lord and putting a veil over his face to prevent its bright shining from frightening his people, but removing the veil when he returned to encounter the Lord. Paul applies this to his present context: "when one [of us] turns to the Lord, the veil [that obscures the full meaning of the old covenant] is removed." And he adds, by way of explanation to help make his interpretative point: "Now the Lord is the Spirit" (2 Cor 3:16–17). In other words, the equivalent to Moses's unveiling to encounter the Lord was, for Paul, the reception of the transforming Spirit. And he ends the analogy with equal boldness:

> And all of us, with unveiled faces, seeing the glory of the Lord as though reflected in a mirror, are being transformed into the same image from one degree of glory to another; for this comes from the Lord, the Spirit. (2 Cor 3:18)

As Luke reminds us, it was the unfettered reception of the Spirit by gentile believers that made it clear to the early Christian leadership that the good news was for gentiles as well, and without any requirement that they should judaize.

The Spirit of Christ

The fact that Paul spoke of the Spirit as *"the Spirit of Christ,"* as we saw in Romans 8:9, and equally could speak of "the Spirit of God," as in Romans 8:14, should not pass without comment. For it means that Paul could think of the Holy Spirit as Christ's Spirit. Jesus was not simply the Messiah who was anointed by the Spirit of God, but that anointing power of God had become so identified with the one anointed that the Spirit of God could be understood as Christ's Spirit. Paul's letter to Rome was written in about the year 56 or 57, and presumably this was not the first time Paul had so identified the Spirit of God with Christ. Which means that well within thirty years of Jesus's ministry, death, and resurrection, God's Spirit was being thought of as "the Spirit of Christ." Similarly in Philippians 1:19 Paul expresses his confidence that "the help of the Spirit of Jesus Christ" would ensure his deliverance. And the implication of the fact that Jesus's distinctive "Abba! Father!" prayer quickly became the distinctive prayer of Paul and his fellow Christians, understood as inspired by the Spirit (Rom 8:16–17; Gal 4:6–7), should not be missed.

What had happened here? Is it simply that Paul was so confident that Jesus had been anointed and empowered by God's Spirit, so that Christ's ministry attested the character of the power that had inspired him? In which case it was as easy to say Jesus's Spirit as it was to say God's Spirit. Was it thus that the Christian concept of God as Trinity first came to expression? Whatever the precise historical details, it cannot be insignificant that Paul so identified the power of Jesus's mission with the Spirit of God that he could quite naturally speak of that power as the Spirit of Christ. Indeed, as we saw in 2 Corinthians 3:12–18, he could identify "the Lord" both with Jesus and with the Spirit. We cannot, of course, infer that Paul had a clear conception of God as Trinity. But it cannot but be significant that he could speak of the same spiritual reality equally in terms of the Lord, the Christ, and the Spirit. Here again Christian theologizing owes an incalculable debt to Paul.

First Installment and Guarantee

The gift of the Spirit to new believers was regarded by Paul as the *first installment* or *guarantee* of the whole process of salvation.[3] Alternatively he refers to the Spirit as the "first fruits" of the harvest of the resurrection of the body when the whole person will be saved (Rom 8:23). As Christ's resurrection was the firstfruits and beginning of the general resurrection (1 Cor 15:20, 23), so the gift of the Spirit was the beginning of the process of redemption that will climax in the resurrection of/from the dead. So the Thessalonian believers could be grateful "because God chose you as the first fruits for salvation through sanctification by the Spirit and

---

3. See particularly 2 Cor 1:22; 5:5. Note also Eph 1:14.

through belief in the truth" (2 Thess 2:13). The Roman believers are reassured that "he who raised Christ from the dead will give life to your mortal bodies also through his Spirit that dwells in you" (Rom 8:11). And Paul gives his own testimony to the Philippian believers before the final reassurance:

> I want to know Christ and the power of his resurrection and the sharing of his sufferings by becoming like him in his death, if somehow I may attain the resurrection from the dead. . . . The Lord Jesus Christ . . . will transform the body of our humiliation that it may be conformed to the body of his glory, by the power that also enables him to make all things subject to himself. (Phil 3:10–11, 20–21)

It should occasion no surprise that Paul thought of the resurrection of Christ in terms of the Spirit: "'The first man, Adam, became a living being'; the last Adam became a life-giving Spirit." And also that he saw the hoped-for resurrection of the body in terms of the Spirit—first the physical body and then the spiritual body (1 Cor 15:42–49). The final work of the Spirit for Paul was the completing of the remaking of humankind into the image of the risen Christ.

Charismatic Community

We have already noted that Paul's most famous way of conceptualizing the worshiping community of Christian believers was as the body of Christ. But in addition, we should not forget that he thought of the congregation of believers as a *charismatic community*. That is, the body of Christians was, like the individual believer, enabled by the Spirit. The gathered congregation could function as the body of Christ only because they had been baptized in the Spirit, and were continually being gifted and enabled by the same Spirit. Paul spends a principal section of his first letter to the Corinthians to make this point with some force (1 Cor 12–14). Christ can be recognized and confessed as Lord only by the enabling and prompting of the Spirit (1 Cor 12:3). It is the gifts of the Spirit, activated by the Spirit, which are the effective functions of the worshiping community (1 Cor 12:2–11). It is worth repeating that for Paul it is by being baptized in the one Spirit that they are all one body, the body of Christ (1 Cor 12:13). And on he goes to describe and instruct the community of Corinthian believers in what it means to be the body of Christ, what it means for the congregation to have worship prompted and led by the Spirit.

The picture of Corinthian worship, and the worship that Paul could assume for the Christian gatherings in Thessalonica (1 Thess 5:19–21) and Rome (Rom 12:6–8), is so different from most Christian experience of worship today that it is little wonder that these passages can be largely ignored by most believers today as referring to a wholly different age remote from our own. An appropriate question might well be whether the Spirit of Jesus is as desired and as welcome as the Spirit and the manifestations of the Spirit evidently were in these early years. If Paul is correct, and the worshiping congregation can function effectively as the body of Christ only through the gifts of the Spirit, only as the Spirit enables members of the congregation to function as members of Christ's body, then it is a fair question to ask: Has modern Christianity, the modern Christian congregation, missed or lost something that Paul clearly regarded as constitutive of the body of Christ? There is no need to try to re-create the Corinthian assembly; would Paul have wanted that? But the question still remains, and remains troubling. Have we Christians lost something in our worship that Paul took for granted as fundamental to being the body of Christ?

Great Expectations

The Parousia and Final Judgment

The hope of Christ's *parousia*, his "coming" again, was a conviction that Paul clearly inherited from the first believers,[4] and it cer-

---

4. "The parousia of the Son of Man" was a prominent theme in the great discourse remembered in Matt 24 (note vv. 3, 27, 37, 39).

tainly was a prominent feature of his letters to the Thessalonians. Christ's expected (soon) coming again had evidently been a major theme in Paul's preaching in Thessalonica (1 Thess 2:19; 3:13). The problem was that some of the Thessalonian believers had died. It is evident from what Paul says that others of the Thessalonian believers feared that those who had died would in consequence be disadvantaged or even miss out at the parousia (1 Thess 4:15). Paul's reassurance was that those who had "fallen asleep" would return with Jesus, when "we who are alive, who are left, will be caught up in the clouds together with them to meet the Lord in the air; and so we will be with the Lord forever" (1 Thess 4:17). Evidently drawing on the memory of Jesus's teaching, Paul reassures his hearers that "the day of the Lord will come like a thief in the night" (1 Thess 5:2).[5] 2 Thessalonians begins with a more stark reaffirmation of the parousia hope—"when the Lord Jesus is revealed from heaven with his mighty angels in flaming fire" (2 Thess 1:7–8)—and proceeds to a bolder exposition of a period of tribulation under the rule of "the lawless one," before deliverance by the Lord Jesus (2 Thess 2:3–11). The later letters do not give such attention to the subject. But Philippians also speaks of "the day of Christ" (Phil 1:6, 10; 2:16), and also echoes 1 Thessalonians 1:10 in speaking of believers "awaiting or expecting" Jesus's return "from heaven" (Phil 3:20).

It should not be forgotten that Paul's theology of salvation not only climaxed in the resurrection of the body, but also included the thought of a final judgment—a final judgment to which believers would be subject, as would all humankind. And Christ would be the judge! Paul does not emphasize this last point very much, but he probably recognized the clear implications of some of Jesus's parables,[6] and in his most intense indictment of human sinfulness in Romans 1–2 he straightforwardly speaks of "the day when, according to my gospel, God, through Jesus Christ, will

---

5. Matt 24:42–44 // Luke 12:39–40.
6. E.g., the wicked tenants (Mark 12:1–12 parr.), the talents (Matt 25:14–30 // Luke 19:11–27), the laborers in the vineyard (Matt 20:1–16), and the rich fool (Luke 12:13–21).

judge the secret thoughts of all" (Rom 2:16). This for Paul was still one of the primary functions of the law—to serve as the measure of God's requirement and judgment. It was "through the law" that "the knowledge of sin" came. And this would be the measure used in the final judgment, "so that . . . the whole world may be held accountable to God" (Rom 3:19). Here again it is striking that Paul did not think of Christ as solely the Savior, and God alone as judge. On the contrary, he could speak equally of "the judgment seat of God" (Rom 14:10) or "the judgment seat of Christ" (2 Cor 5:10). Indeed, one of his favorite phrases was "the day of the Lord" as indicating the day of judgment,[7] a prospect which he could confront with some assurance (1 Cor 3:10–15).

The Tension between Already and Not Yet

One of the most distinctive features of Paul's understanding of the salvation which his gospel proffered was what can be described as the already/not-yet tension. This was the twofold conviction: first, that something had already happened for the believer, and second, that salvation was not yet complete. This, of course, was a conscious mirroring of what Paul regarded as the twofoldedness of Jesus's ministry. Jesus had already, during his ministry, or should we say, his first ministry, begun the process of salvation. His death and resurrection brought into effect through faith the beginning of the saving process—hence the "already." But that process would not be completed until the return of Christ, "not yet," but in Paul's hope, soon. As again he spelled out his confident hope in his first letter to the Corinthian believers: "As all die in Adam, so all will be made alive in Christ . . . Christ the first fruits, then at his coming those who belong to Christ" (1 Cor 15:22–23).

But in between that beginning and the triumphant climax was the process of transformation to become like Christ, to transfer, as it were, from being primarily "in Adam" to being fully "in Christ." In between was the process of being trans-

---

7. 1 Cor 1:8; 5:5; 2 Cor 1:14; 1 Thess 5:2; 2 Thess 2:2.

formed to become like Christ. As Paul puts it most strikingly in Philippians 3:10–11: "I want to know Christ and the power of his resurrection and the sharing of his sufferings by becoming like him in his death, if somehow I may attain the resurrection from the dead."

The fact that he can put knowing "the power of Christ's resurrection" prior to "the sharing of his sufferings" presumably indicates that Paul saw the two as inextricably intertwined. The "already" was not the complete story or the complete process, but the "first installment," which, as we have seen, was the gift of the Spirit, in itself the guarantee that the process begun would surely be completed. So Paul can describe the process as one of being transformed from one degree of glory to another into the image of Christ (2 Cor 3:18), of being conformed to the image of God's Son (Rom 8:29), "to the body of his glory."[8] There is a counterpart to reception of the spirit of adoption (Rom 8:15), which is the further act of adoption, namely, the redemption of the body (Rom 8:23). The gift of the Spirit is the reassurance that the process of salvation will be completed.

Jesus as Lord

As we have seen, Paul does not hesitate to speak of Jesus as *Lord*. Of course, he was well aware that *kyrios* (Lord) was the Greek translation of the Hebrew, "Yahweh." But what is striking is that he was quite happy to take references to Yahweh and refer them to the Lord Jesus—as in Romans 10:9–13, citing Joel 2:32: "Everyone who calls upon the name of the Lord shall be saved." Very striking too is the fact that Paul draws on one of the strongest monotheistic passages in the whole Bible—Isaiah 45:21–23—and uses its final acclamation, "To me every knee shall bow, every tongue shall swear," in his great hymn of praise to Christ (Phil 2:6–11). And in Romans 9:5 Paul's Greek (or punctuation) can be taken as Paul referring to Christ as God "who is over all." Paul

---

8. Phil 3:21; cf. 1 Cor 15:49.

certainly saw God as fully acting in and through Christ. He freely applied references to Yahweh in the Hebrew Bible to Christ. "In him," he did not hesitate to assert in another hymn, "all the fullness of God was pleased to dwell" (Col 1:19). Indeed, the hymn begins by hailing Christ as "the image of the invisible God, the firstborn of all creation," in whom "all things in heaven and on earth were created," "created through him and for him. He himself is before all things, and in him all things hold together" (Col 1:15–17). Wow! How can we refrain from acknowledging that Paul saw in Christ the agency of creation itself. It looks very much, then, that Paul was so convinced that God had acted through Christ that he did not hold back on some occasions from identifying Christ with God.

However, when he applied himself to more detail of what believers could hope for, he expressed himself more carefully, as we see in 1 Corinthians 15:24–28. This is one of the most extraordinary expressions of Paul's confident hope—hope not just for the future, but for the final future, the climax of human history, in which (of course, for Paul) Christ has the climactic role. But what is most striking is that the climax is not so much Christ, but God.

> Then comes the end, when he [Christ] hands over the kingdom to God the Father. . . . For he must reign until he has put all his enemies under his feet. . . . For "God has put all things in subjection under his feet" [Ps 8:7]. But when it says, "All things are put in subjection," it is plain that this does not include the one who put all things in subjection under him. When all things are subjected to him, then the Son himself will also be subjected to the one who put all things in subjection under him, so that God may be all in all. (1 Cor 15:24–28)

The really striking feature is that the language Paul uses for creation in relation to Christ is the same language he uses for the Son's relation to God—"subjection": as "all things" are put in subjection under God, so Jesus the Son will also be subject to God. In the end Christ will "hand over the kingdom" to God. Which must mean that, however highly Paul revered Jesus, he remained a faithful monotheist. The climax is God.

The Later Paul

Most scholars think that the later letters attributed to Paul, particularly the Pastoral Epistles,[9] were not written by Paul himself, but by one or another of those who followed him. Alternatively, if Paul had survived his imprisonment in Rome (where Acts ends its account of Christianity's beginnings), conceivably he could have written further letters. In fact, the issue of authorship as such may not be very important, since we can hardly exclude the possibility that Paul himself had developed, for example, in his views of churchmanship to include bishops (*episkopoi*)[10] and deacons (1 Tim 3:8, 12) in the ordering of the churches he had established. Either way, the Pastorals are probably best taken as indicating how the Pauline tradition developed in the later decades of the first century.

What is more important here is whether the gospel of Paul and the way in which Jesus was remembered and portrayed in the Pastorals are any different. The talk is still of Christ's predetermined appearing to fulfill God's purpose of salvation:

> This grace was given to us in Christ Jesus before the ages began, but it has now been revealed through the appearing of our Savior Christ Jesus, who abolished death and brought life and immortality to light through the gospel. (2 Tim 1:9–10)

Titus 1:2–3 speaks of "the hope of eternal life that God, who never lies, promised before the ages began" and is now revealed in the

9. 1 Timothy, 2 Timothy, and Titus.

10. Since the first reference in the Pauline letters is plural, *episkopoi* in Philippians should probably be better translated as "overseers" (Phil 1:1). In 1 Tim 3:2 and Titus 1:7, passages dealing with church order, the reference is singular (*episkopos*) and "bishop" would be a more appropriate translation.

proclamation of Christ. Titus 2:13, however, raises the intriguing question whether the writer was already willing to speak of Jesus as God ("our great God and Savior, Jesus Christ"); or should we rather translate "the great God and our Savior Jesus Christ"? The issue is perhaps clarified when we take the full phrase, "the manifestation of the glory of our great God and Savior"—Jesus's coming being seen as the manifestation of the glory of the one God. The parallel with John 1:14 ("we have seen his glory . . .") suggests that both the Pastorals and John were moving in the same direction in their appreciation of the significance of Jesus.

The title "Savior" is much more prominent in the Pastorals than in the earlier Pauline letters, and is used equally of Christ as it is of God—especially in Titus: "God our Savior" (Titus 1:3; 2:10; 3:4) and "Christ Jesus our Savior" (Titus 1:4; 2:13; 3:6). And, interestingly, the talk of the second appearing has already assumed the more measured tones of a hope which no longer expects imminent fulfillment. The audience is charged "to keep the commandment without spot or blame until the manifestation of our Lord Jesus Christ, which he will bring about at the right time" (1 Tim 6:14–15). The day of his appearing is still looked forward to, but without any note of urgency (2 Tim 4:1, 8). There is more concern that lives be lived responsibly "in the present age . . . while we wait for the blessed hope" to be realized (Titus 2:12–13).

But otherwise, the Christology is characteristically contained in what were evidently already well-established creedal and hymnic formulae, often referred to as "faithful sayings":[11]

1 Tim 1:15   "The saying is sure and worthy of full acceptance, that Christ Jesus came into the world to save sinners—of whom I am the foremost."

1 Tim 2:5–6   "There is one God; there is one mediator between God and humankind, Christ Jesus, himself human, who gave himself a ransom for all."

11. See also 1 Tim 3:1; 4:9.

1 Tim 3:16   "He was revealed in flesh, vindicated in spirit, seen by angels, proclaimed among Gentiles, believed in throughout the world, taken up in glory."

1 Tim 6:13   "In the presence of God, who gives life to all things, and of Christ Jesus, who in his testimony before Pontius Pilate made the good confession."

2 Tim 2:8   "Remember Jesus Christ, raised from the dead, a descendant of David—that is my gospel, for which I suffer hardship."

2 Tim 2:11–13 "The saying is sure: If we have died with him, we will also live with him; if we endure, we will also reign with him; if we deny him, he will also deny us; if we are faithless, he remains faithful—for he cannot deny himself."

Titus 3:5–8   "He saved us, not because of any works of righteousness that we had done, but according to his mercy, through the water of rebirth and renewal by the Holy Spirit. This Spirit he poured out on us richly through Jesus Christ our Savior, so that, having been justified by his grace, we might become heirs according to the hope of eternal life. The saying is sure."

This is presumably what is summed up as "the teaching that is in accordance with godliness" (1 Tim 6:3).

This is probably what we should expect in a second-generation view of Christ, where faith had become more established and enshrined in formulae ("faithful sayings") which summarized the beliefs at the center of their worship and which provided the basis for their lives individually and communally. Here we can see the way still-early belief about Christ was developing toward the more elaborate and more carefully defined con-

JESUS ACCORDING TO THE NEW TESTAMENT

victions about Jesus which eventuated in the classic Christian creeds. That such developments could be attributed to Paul, or at the very least to the influence of Paul, is a reminder of just how much earliest Christianity's appreciation of Christ owed to Paul.

*　　*　　*

It is quite amazing just how much Christianity's self-understanding and understanding of Jesus owe to Paul. It is not just the question, Without Paul, would the Jesus movement ever have penetrated far into Europe? We might reframe the same question as, Without Paul, would the Jesus movement ever have become Christianity as it has been understood for nineteen centuries? And integral to that latter question is the issue of the way Jesus was coming to be understood. And here is where we see the lasting influence of Paul on Christian theology.

- It is first with Paul that the Christian gospel was summed up and worked out, not in terms of Jesus's teaching, but as focused on Jesus's death as the decisive atonement for sins, and on Jesus's resurrection as the sure promise of a salvation which would be complete and final.
- It is first with Paul that the gospel could be summed up in terms of a justification and an acceptance by God which depended solely on a trust in the gospel and in the one whom the gospel portrayed.
- It is first with Paul that the benefits offered to faith in Christ could be understood as a participation in Christ, both in what he did in his death and resurrection and in living out daily life "with Christ" and "in Christ."
- It is first with Paul that the gift of the Spirit is understood to be the defining mark of the Christian.
- And it is first with Paul that the hope held out to believers is not only of Christ's return, but of becoming more and more like Christ, until finally transformed or raised again, as modeled by Christ, the firstfruits of the final harvest of salvation.

In the later Paul we see the radical redefining of Christ for a much wider audience carried through—a more conformist Paul, with his radical edge trimmed and his ecclesiology more formally structured and amenable to control once he had gone to his reward. But his own radicalness could not be forgotten, such had been his influence in spreading Christianity well beyond Palestine and Syria. His letters with their often pointed instructions were evidently considered to be of enduring importance well beyond the particular churches to which he wrote. And so, almost inevitably, they were the first and most obvious candidates, along with the records of Jesus's ministry, to be included in the canon which became the New Testament—the beginning of the Christian Scripture. It remains of first importance for Christianity that the ecclesiology of the Pastoral Epistles did not result in these alone of the Pauline heritage being counted as Scripture, that the enduring impact of the early Paul was not lost to sight in what is generally known as the "early Catholicism" of the later New Testament period. Christian history has put Peter next to Jesus in a Christian hierarchy of the most influential historical figures in the originating of Christianity. And Peter's ecclesiological influence is clear in the dominance of Rome in Christian history. But Paul carries much more weight in the New Testament canon than does Peter. And next to Jesus, it is the Pauline heritage which has been the re-creative force in Christianity, we might even say from the Reformation onwards. It is the Paul who broke through old boundaries and encouraged the life of the Spirit to go on bubbling and bursting forth in new forms and formulae who most serves Christianity today, as in the mission which he gave his life to fulfilling.[12]

12. For further detail and discussion, please see James D. G. Dunn, *The Theology of Paul the Apostle* (Grand Rapids: Eerdmans, 1998); and Dunn, *Beginning from Jerusalem*, vol. 2 of *Christianity in the Making* (Grand Rapids: Eerdmans, 2009).

CHAPTER SEVEN

Jesus according to

Hebrews

W hen we turn to the letter to the Hebrews, it quickly appears to be a somewhat strange new territory. It is not just the name, "To the Hebrews." Why "the Hebrews"? Why not "to Jews" or "Jews of the diaspora" (scattered round the Mediterranean)? But more important, we do not know who wrote the letter. Traditionally it was attributed to Paul, and was still so in the King James (Authorized) Version of the Bible published in 1611. But the letter itself gives no indication as to who wrote it, and guesses, like Barnabas, have no substantive ground on which to build their answer. How, then, did it make it into the New Testament canon? Part of the answer may be that it is generally reckoned to be the finest Greek composition within the New Testament. But the principal reason must be that it was making a substantial impact in many churches round the Mediterranean. Indeed, it has strong parallels to the thought world of Alexandrian Judaism, familiar to us from the intertestamental Wisdom of Solomon and the Alexandrian Jewish philosopher Philo. So perhaps it was the clearest expression of early Alexandrian Christianity to emerge in the Mediterranean world, and partly as a result was widely appreciated around the Mediterranean churches. Which could suggest that the author was Apollos, who came from Alexandria and who evidently was proficient in Greek rhetoric (Acts 18:24). But we are too much in the dark in all this, and the little patch of light around Apollos could be misleading. So we simply have to accept that Hebrews was widely received and influential as a well-considered expression of earliest Christian belief. In any case, the view of Jesus presented there has a distinctive character that supplements the more straightforward portrayals of the synoptic evangelists and the more sophisticated portrayals of John and Paul.

Whatever the details of its origin and authorship, the fact remains that the letter became an established part of the New Testament—and that despite the fact, as we shall see below, that what we may call its churchmanship is somewhat at odds with the ecclesiology that became the norm for Christianity during the second century. In fact, however, the portrayal of Christ in Hebrews is as rich and as varied as what we found in Paul's letters.

Christ as Wisdom

The letter, if it is properly to be called a letter, opens with a striking assertion, probably drawing on an early Christian hymn:

> In times past God spoke to the fathers through the prophets
> at many times and in diverse ways.
> But in these last days he spoke to us through a Son,
>> whom he appointed heir of all things,
>> through whom also he made the world,
>> who is the radiance of God's glory
>> and the stamp of his very being,
>> sustaining all things by his word of power.
> Having made purification for sins, he sat down at the right
> hand of the majesty on high. (Heb 1:1–3)

The hymn is a striking expression of Wisdom Christology, not dissimilar to what we saw in Colossians 1:15–20. Noticeable is the use of "radiance" (*apaugasma*), which may allude to Wisdom of Solomon 7:26, where, in a powerful description, divine Wisdom is described as the "radiance of eternal light" (the only occurrence of the word in the LXX).

The echoes of Philo are even stronger. One of his tractates, on Genesis 15:2–18, is entitled *Who Is the Heir of Divine Things?* The *second* line of the Hebrews hymn ("through whom also he made the world") is very similar to what Philo says of the Logos (Word) in several passages.[1] Philo also speaks of man's mind or soul as the *apaugasma* of the divine Logos.[2] And he speaks frequently of the human soul as receiving a "stamp" of divine power,[3] or being itself the "stamp/impression" of the Logos.[4]

The point is that in Hebrew thought Wisdom and Logos were ways of speaking about God's action upon and within the world of space-time. It is clear from various passages that for Philo the Logos was "the reasoning faculty of God in the act of planning to create the universe,"[5] or the archetypal divine idea which came to expression in creation, above all of humankind.[6] As noted above in chapter 3, part of the attraction of the term *logos* was that it could express both the unspoken word and the spoken word. So the concept of divine Logos could express what we might refer to both as the inner intention of God and its expression in action. For Philo, in other words, the divine Logos was the thought of God coming to expression—which well explains the attraction of the term to the evangelist John. On this point one of the most significant passages in Philo is *On Dreams* 1.65–66, where he envisages penetrating as far as possible into the divine Word, only to realize that in doing so "he does not actually reach him who is in very essence God, but sees him from afar."

---

1. *On the Sacrifices of Cain and Abel* 8; *That God Is Unchangeable* 57; *On the Migration of Abraham* 6; *On the Special Laws* 1.8.

2. *On the Creation of the World* 146; *On the Special Laws* 1.8.

3. *Allegorical Interpretation* 1.61; *On the Sacrifices of Cain and Abel* 60; *That the Worse Attacks the Better* 77; *On the Confusion of Tongues* 102; *Who Is the Heir?* 38, 181, 294.

4. *Allegorical Interpretation* 3.95–97.

5. *On the Creation of the World* 24.

6. *On the Creation of the World* 139; *On Drunkenness* 32–33; *Who Is the Heir?* 230–31; *On Dreams* 2.45; *Questions and Answers on Genesis* 1.4; *Questions and Answers on Exodus* 2.122.

Similarly with Wisdom, the much more popular category among Israel's wisdom writers. As again, for example, in Proverbs 3:19: "The LORD by wisdom founded the earth; by understanding he established the heavens." The author of the Wisdom of Solomon (9:1–6) prays:

> O God of my fathers and Lord of mercy,
> who hast made all things by thy word,
> and by thy wisdom hast formed man, . . .
> give me the wisdom that sits by thy throne. . . .
> For even if one is perfect among the sons of men,
> yet without the wisdom that comes from thee
> he will be regarded as nothing.

And Sirach ends with a thought similar to that of Philo on the Logos: "Though we speak much we cannot reach the end, and the sum of our words is: 'He is the all'" (Sir 43:27). In other words, Wisdom and Logos are simply ways of speaking about God's ordering of creation, and also of indicating God's design for humankind in the law.[7]

Here Christian thinkers need to remember that Israel's conception of God was almost as complicated and refined as the Christian understanding of God. God's interaction with the cosmos and with humankind could be spoken of in terms of God's Spirit, of divine Logos and divine Wisdom, all the while recognizing that God as such was always well beyond human comprehension. As we have seen, Philo makes this clear when he envisages going as far as he can in his conception of God, only to realize there is much further to go. The Logos and Wisdom are as much as it is possible for human beings to know God; but, of course, there is far more which is beyond human knowledge and perception. This was precisely why Wisdom and Logos were so attractive to the first Christian theologians. Hebrew reflection had found Wisdom in particular to be an effective way of speaking about

---

7. See further my *Christology in the Making*, 2nd ed. (Grand Rapids: Eerdmans, 1999), chs. 6 and 7.

God's interaction with creation and involvement with his people, without compromising his transcendence, and without compromising their belief that God was one. It was undoubtedly this which prompted the Wisdom Christology in Paul, as we saw in the hymn Paul quotes in Colossians 1:15–20, and in Hebrews 1, as also the Logos Christology of John's prologue (John 1:1–18). It is a somewhat uncomfortable thought that Israel's Wisdom tradition and Philo's Logos reflection managed to maintain a spontaneity and flexibility which the Christian adaptation of it in Christology quite quickly lost.

God's Son

That powerful opening of the letter, quoted above at the beginning of the chapter, moves on immediately to another powerful affirmation. For it ends by noting that the Son had become much superior to angels (Heb 1:4). And, as though the preceding statement did not provide sufficient explanation, the author adds the explanation of the Son's superiority (Heb 1:5–6):

> For to which of the angels did God ever say, "You are my Son; today I have begotten you" [Ps 2:7]? Or again, "I will be his Father, and he will be my Son" [2 Sam 7:14]? And again, when he brings the firstborn into the world, he says, "Let all God's angels worship him" [Deut 32:43].

And he proceeds through a sequence of biblical quotations (Heb 1:7–12) to indicate that the Son is high above the angels, ending with the climactic question (Heb 1:13): "To which of the angels has he ever said, 'Sit at my right hand until I make your enemies a footstool for your feet'?" (Ps 110:1).

Israel's Psalms had still much more to feed into Hebrews' Christology. For, still pursuing the theme of the Son's superiority to angels, the author of Hebrews goes on to reflect on Psalm 8 (Heb 2:5–9)—here drawing in his own adaptation of the "Son of Man" Christology so familiar from the Gospels: "What is man that you are mindful of him, or the son of man that you care for him?" The psalmist had gloried in humankind's place in creation, the climax of creation, "a little lower than the angels," "crowned with glory and honor," with "all things [in subjection] under their feet" (Ps 8:5–6). In Paul's use of Psalm 8:6 the assurance was that by raising Jesus from the dead God had exalted Jesus, and that God would indeed "put all things in subjection under his feet" (1 Cor 15:27). Hebrews notes that in fact Psalm 8:6 was not true, or should we say, not yet true, that all things were in subjection to humans. What we do see, however, is Jesus, "who for a little while was made lower than the angels, now crowned with glory and honor because of the suffering of death, so that by the grace of God he might taste death for everyone" (Heb 2:9). In other words, it is Jesus who first really fulfills God's purpose for humankind as a whole. But he does so (Heb 2:10–13) as one with those who can be called both his "brothers and sisters" (Ps 22:22) and his "children" (Isa 8:18).

What Hebrews celebrates, then, is that Jesus shared fully the reality and frailness of humankind, "so that through death he might destroy the one who has the power of death, that is, the devil, and free those who all their lives were held in slavery by the fear of death" (Heb 2:14–15). This is one of the most powerful passages in Hebrews, not least since it takes seriously Jesus's humanness even while celebrating his superiority over angels. It is one of the most striking transitions in the document. Having begun by stressing Jesus's superiority to angels, the author points in another direction: "For it is clear that he did not come to help angels, but the descendants of Abraham" (Heb 2:16). Angels do not need salvation. It is human beings that need a savior. That was why "he had to become like his brothers in every respect, so that he might be a merciful and faithful high priest in the service of God, to make a sacrifice of atonement for the sins of the people. Because he himself was tested by what he suffered, he is able to help those who are being tested" (Heb 2:17–18). That is why his superiority to angels is not to the point here. And why, having introduced the theme of Jesus as high priest, the author pauses to press home the point that Jesus, "the apostle and high priest of our confession" (Heb 3:1), was superior also to Moses, the most highly revered servant of God within Israel's history and cult. "Moses was faithful . . . as a servant. . . . Christ, however, was faithful . . . as a son" (Heb 3:5–6).

At which point the writer pauses and invites those listening to the reading of his letter also to pause and to reflect on their responsibility in receiving such a message. As the Israelites themselves had failed so badly, in failing to enter the promised land, so too the listeners to the letter being read to them should take care not to repeat the Israelites' mistake, not to harden their hearts, but to "hear his voice" (Heb 3:7, 15; 4:7). And only then does the writer turn to his main theme.

Priest according to the Order of Melchizedek

It is at Hebrews 4:14 that the letter opens up its main theme. In Jesus, the Son of God, we have a great high priest. The important thing about the high priest is that he is one of us. He is not above and unfamiliar with the human weaknesses which we all experience. Like us, Jesus has been tested. Yet, unlike us, he is without sin (Heb 4:15). The usual high priest "is able to deal gently with the ignorant and wayward, since he himself is subject to weakness; and because of this he must offer sacrifice for his own sins as well as for those of the people" (Heb 5:2–3). Not so with Jesus.

For Jesus's priesthood is different from the regular priesthood. To make his point the writer goes back once again to Psalm 110, from which he has already drawn the proof that Jesus is higher than the angels (Heb 1:13). Not only is Jesus hailed as God's Son (Heb 5:5, again citing Ps 2:7), but Psalm 110:4 also declares him "a priest forever, according to the order of Melchizedek" (Heb 5:6). Which does not mean that he was exempt from suffering. On the contrary, "although he was a Son, he learned obedience through what he suffered; and having [thus] been made perfect, he became the source of eternal salvation for all who obey him, having been designated by God a high priest according to the order of Melchizedek" (Heb 5:8–10). This is most striking, that Hebrews recognizes and emphasizes the humanity of Jesus—"he learned obedience," and it was through his suffering that he was made perfect. The author could hardly stress more clearly that Jesus had been able to accomplish what he had accomplished only through his suffering and death.

After another pause to warn against backsliding (Heb 6:1–8), the author takes up the symbolism of the sanctuary. As his audience would know, the tent of meeting during Israel's wilderness wanderings had had two sections: the holy place where the priests could enter daily to offer the blood of the everyday sacrifices, and the holy of holies. Only the high priest could enter into the holy of holies, and only on one day in the year, the most sacred Day of Atonement, when he would sprinkle the blood of the atoning goat on "the mercy seat" to make atonement "for himself and for his house and for all the assembly of Israel" (Lev 16:17). It is this imagery which the writer of Hebrews takes up, seeing the tent of meeting as an image of heaven, of the very presence of God. As the high priest entered the holy of holies with the blood of the atoning sacrifice, so Christ, high priest according to the order of Melchizedek, had entered heaven, "behind the curtain" separating the holy place from the holy of holies, "a forerunner on our behalf" (Heb 6:19–20), to open the way for ordinary humans to enter, that is, as will become apparent, to enter on their own behalf.

All this depends on the writer's understanding of Melchizedek and of what Scripture says about him. As Genesis 14:18 indicates, Melchizedek was king of Salem, usually taken to be Jerusalem,[8] and "priest of God Most High." According to the Genesis account, Melchizedek met Abraham and blessed him. Significantly Abraham acknowledged Melchizedek's priesthood and the blessing Melchizedek had bestowed on him by giving Melchizedek a tithe, "one-tenth of everything" (Gen 14:20). The most significant thing about Melchizedek, for the writer of Hebrews, however, is not only that his name means "king of righteousness," and, as king of Salem, "king of peace" (Heb 7:2). What is more significant is that

---

8. Somewhat surprisingly, the author of Hebrews shows no interest in this point; it is the heavenly Jerusalem in which he is more interested (Heb 12:22).

the very limited amount of information which Genesis has about Melchizedek allows the author of Hebrews to conclude that the Melchizedek of Genesis 14 was "without father, without mother, without genealogy, having neither beginning of days nor end of life" (Heb 7:3). It is a very bold deduction to make: that because Melchizedek's birth and death are not recorded in the scriptural history, he can be counted as symbolizing or representing something eternal. As a priest, without (recorded) beginning and end of days, he can represent an eternal priesthood; "resembling the Son of God, he remains a priest forever" (Heb 7:3). And the fact that Abraham paid Melchizedek tithes, and received his blessing, means that all Abraham's descendants, including the priestly descendants of Levi, acknowledge that the Melchizedek priesthood is superior to the Levitical priesthood (Heb 7:4–10).

With the bit now between his teeth, the writer goes on to draw out the significance of the Melchizedek line of priesthood (Heb 7:11–28). In particular, priests according to the order of Aaron die; their priesthood is not forever (Heb 7:23). And they have to offer sacrifices every day, for their own sins as well (Heb 7:27). In contrast, Christ is a priest, not by virtue of physical descent (from Levi), "but through the power of an indestructible life" (Heb 7:16). As Psalm 110:4 affirms, "You are a priest forever, according to the order of Melchizedek," an authorization for Christ's priesthood cited twice within a few verses (Heb 7:17, 21), no doubt to make the point clear. And, unlike the Aaronic priests, Christ does not need to offer sacrifices every day, for his own sins as well as for the sins of the people. In contrast, he has done it, that is, offered sacrifice for the sins of the people, "once for all when he offered himself" (Heb 7:27).

Having argued his case for claiming that Christ is a priest— unqualified as not coming from the tribe of Levi, but qualified by resurrection and ascension for the eternal priesthood of Melchizedek—the writer emphasizes that this accords with the promise of a new covenant (Heb 8). The problem with the first covenant was that the offerings for sins had to take place every day in an earthly sanctuary. But the promise of a new covenant (Jer 31:31–34) includes the promise that sins will be forgiven once and for all

(Heb 8:12). Which means that repeated offerings for sins are now no longer necessary. The "new covenant" has rendered the old covenant "obsolete" (Heb 8:13). And the author goes on to contrast the old tabernacle (and the Jerusalem temple) with its holy place, and curtained-off holy of holies, with the real presence of God in heaven, where Christ has entered in his ascension. He has fulfilled the climactic role of priest, bringing not the blood of goats and calves, but his own blood, "thus obtaining eternal redemption" (Heb 9:12). And whereas the old covenant priests had to offer sacrifices repeatedly, day by day, year by year, Jesus has entered the heavenly reality, into the very presence of God, "once for all" offering his own blood. It is from there that Jesus will appear a second time, not to deal with sin (he has already done that), "but to save those who are eagerly waiting for him" (Heb 9:28).

The author of Hebrews has already made his point, but he goes on in chapter 10 to drive it home. The essential point is that since Christ has secured the forgiveness of sins, by his once-for-all self-sacrifice on the cross, "there is no longer any offering for sin," no more need for such offerings (Heb 10:18). By his death on the cross Jesus has breached the curtain which had shielded the holy of holies, the symbolic presence of God, from everyday human eyes. In consequence, the great climax is that we too, author and recipients of the letter, now can have confidence to enter the (heavenly) sanctuary by the blood of Jesus. The curtain separating the holy place from the holy of holies has been stripped away. Now we all, no longer just priests, and no longer just the high priest, can press through into the heavenly holy of holies, into the very presence of God for ourselves (Heb 10:19–22). For those whose whole lives and religious understanding and experience had been built round the assumption that God is so infinite and holy that only one person, and only once a year, could enter his presence, Hebrews must have been read and listened to with something of a shock. The writer's whole point was and is that Jesus has changed everything. He himself has more than fulfilled all the requirements necessary to complete the role of priest. In fulfilling the role of definitive sacrifice as well as that of sacrificing priest, he has stripped away the curtain that shielded the presence of God from human eyes. And in doing so he has opened the way for those previously prevented from experiencing God's forgiveness and presence directly for themselves, has opened the way into God's very presence.

It is quite a puzzling fact that Hebrews was accepted into the New Testament canon, at a time when the language and practice of priesthood were coming back into early Christianity. What is equally puzzling is the fact that the Second Vatican Council used Hebrews, of all texts, to expound the doctrine of a continuing special order of priesthood within the people of God. To use Hebrews to justify or explain a Christian priesthood, while ignoring the clear thrust and argument of the letter as a whole (as does Vatican II's *Lumen Gentium* §28), still seems to me to constitute a form of *eis*egesis (reading into the text) and special pleading which has no justification from tradition. The letter could hardly be clearer: (1) Jesus's priesthood is unique and unrepeatable— only those are qualified who have "neither beginning of days nor end of life." That is, only one qualifies for that unique Melchizedek priesthood—only Jesus. And (2) because he has opened the way to God, so that worshipers can approach God immediately and directly, there is no longer any need for priests to play an intermediary role—the need for the role Christ played has ended. This is precisely the wonder and excitement of Hebrews's argument: that the worshiper through Christ has immediate and direct access to the presence of God, without requiring any priestly intermediation. This is the lasting significance of Hebrews! Somewhat sadly, it is hard to escape the conclusion that to return to a system of worship still requiring and dependent on priestly mediation would seem to reject Hebrews and in effect to dismiss it from the New Testament!

The Pioneer and Perfecter of Faith

The author's argument is more or less complete, so after a word of encouragement (Heb 10:24–25) and a rather more frightening word of warning (Heb 10:26–39), he turns to a final paean in praise of faith and the history of faith. It starts with a striking definition of faith—striking, not least, because it lifts readers' and hearers' eyes beyond the usual Christian definition of faith as believing in Christ. Here faith is defined as "the assurance of things hoped for, the conviction of things not seen" (Heb 11:1). Here is a definition which allows believers in Christ to acknowledge fellowship with a much wider circle of faith. In particular, it enables Christians to recognize a continuity of belief in Christ with a broader or perhaps deeper trust which those who never knew Christ nevertheless exercised in relation to God, even if less clearly known than Christ had made possible. It is worth noting the high respect which Hebrews shows to this not-yet-Christian faith. Hebrews 11:1 encourages Christians to recognize fully the character and quality of genuine faith and trust in God where Jesus Christ has never been known.

The list of honorable mention begins with Abel (Heb 11:4–6), concentrates naturally on Abraham (Heb 11:8–19) and Moses (Heb 11:23–29), and runs out of breath already at Israel's judges. It climaxes with the recognition, already implicit in the opening definition of faith, that despite such impressive faith, their experience fell short, since it was not yet—and could not yet be—faith in Christ (Heb 11:39–40). But this roll call of faith was all the preparation needed for the climax of faith, faith in Christ. The powerful image is of a long-distance race, which the author and readers of/ listeners to his letter are running, with the supporting crowd made up of those cited who have already completed the race. And the goal, the finishing line, is already in sight, signaled by Jesus, "the pioneer and perfecter of our faith, who for the sake of the joy that was set before him, endured the cross . . . and has taken his seat at the right hand of the throne of God" (Heb 12:2).

Further exhortation climaxes in a contrast between the mountain in Sinai where Moses encountered God (Heb 12:18–21) and Mount Zion, the heavenly Jerusalem, to which those addressed in the letter have already come. That is where "God the judge of all" is, together with "the spirits of the righteous made perfect," and also, most important, Jesus, "the mediator of a new covenant" whose "sprinkled blood . . . speaks a better word than the blood of Abel" (Heb 12:22–24). Still more exhortation climaxes in the thought that "Jesus Christ is the same yesterday and today and forever"—an enduring mediator and through-way to God which leaves tabernacle, and temple priest and cult, far in the past (Heb 13:8). The memory of Israel's cult provision of sacrifice for sin does not entice back to that provision, for it simply pointed forward to Jesus, who "also suffered outside the city gate in order to sanctify the people by his own blood" (Heb 13:12). So believers in Jesus should not allow the ties of family and location to hold them back, but should be prepared for insult and abuse. They should remember and take heart from the fact that their primary loyalty is no longer to a city to which they belong or a tradition to which they were formerly indebted. "Here we have no lasting city, but we are looking for the city that is to come"—a new Jerusalem (Heb 13:14)!

And the writer ends with one of the most powerful parting blessings in the whole of biblical and Christian tradition:

> Now may the God of peace, who brought back from the dead our Lord Jesus, the great shepherd of the sheep, by the blood of the eternal covenant, make you complete in everything good so that you may do his will, working among us that which is pleasing in his sight, through Jesus Christ, to whom be the glory forever and ever. Amen. (Heb 13:20–21)

*   *   *

When we look at the letter to the Hebrews as we have done, it is difficult to avoid a feeling of some surprise that the letter is part of the New Testament canon. The quality of its Greek and possibly its somewhat exceptional origin in Egypt (if that is where it came from) presumably played a part. And, as already noted, we have to assume that it made an extensive and enduring impact round the Mediterranean churches—otherwise it is difficult to account for its acceptance. But apart from that we are in the dark.

The striking thing is that this acceptance must have been growing and becoming established precisely at the time when, presumably as a result of the influence of Clement, Ignatius, and others, the role of the priest was becoming reestablished in the Christian churches. We have to add: becoming reestablished *despite* Hebrews. For if we have properly understood Hebrews, it would have been most natural to conclude that the worshipers of Jesus no longer needed priests. Christ himself was the only priest now needed. All could go directly, for themselves, into the presence of God. But, despite Hebrews, the centrality of priests as intermediaries and essential to effective worship was reaffirmed in second-century Christianity—and quickly became established, again despite Hebrews. Quite how Hebrews could be so prized (as to become canonical) and yet at the same time could be so ignored (by the reaffirmation that priests are still necessary for legitimate worship of the God and Father of our Lord Jesus Christ) is one of the great puzzles in the early history of Christianity.

What is also so surprising is that early rabbinic Judaism was at the same time moving in precisely the opposite direction. With the destruction of Jerusalem and of the Jerusalem temple (the very heart of traditional Judaism), and despite the longing for the temple's restoration (still an ache in the heart of many Jews), Judaism moved forward in a new and different direction. The temple ceased to be the focus of Judaism. The Torah became the almost exclusive focus of rabbinic Judaism. The priest lost his central function in Jewish religion. Now the rabbi took over the central role. And this was happening at precisely the same time that early Christianity was turning again to religious belief and practice in which the priest was central.

This always strikes me as one of the most astonishing developments of the late first and early second century in the two religions closest to the heart of Jesus and the first disciples. Despite its long history of being a temple-centered religion, with priests and sacrifices so fundamental to the religion that the religion could hardly be conceived without priest and sacrifice, Judaism became something different from the second century onwards—a religion of book (Torah) and teacher (rabbi), no longer of priest and sacrifice. In contrast—indeed in complete contrast—Christianity began with a focus on the word which Jesus preached and embodied, with priest and sacrifice not at all at the center; and yet in the second century Christianity reverted to the concept and practice of religion as focused on priest and sacrifice. The Lord's Supper was in effect transformed from being part of a shared meal into a reenactment of a priestly sacrifice. Whereas in Judaism priestly ritual gave way to word expounded, in Christianity the word became in effect subordinated to the revived priestly ritual.

One cannot but wonder what the author of the letter to the Hebrews would have made of it all—and indeed how a Christian priest today can expound and explain Hebrews without at least some, and perhaps considerable, embarrassment.

CHAPTER EIGHT

Jesus according to

James, Peter, John, and Jude

L etters seem to have been the principal form of communication between the founding leaders of earliest Christianity and the churches they established. Nor should we forget that the final book of the New Testament, Revelation, as we shall see, is in effect prefaced with a sequence of letters. Since no microphones or recording equipment was available to preserve the sermons, addresses, or teaching which brought into existence the churches addressed in these letters, we are dependent solely on the letters themselves to gain at least a glimpse of the churches to which they were written. Equally we have to depend on various echoes and allusions to gain an impression of the good news in response to which the churches came into existence. Here we lack the assistance which Luke's account of the early spread of Christianity through the mission of Paul provided in giving what we might call a two-dimensional perspective on the Pauline churches. But at least we have the letters of James, Peter, John, and Jude themselves, and can gain from them a fuller impression of and insight into Christianity's beginnings apart from the Pauline mission, on which, as just noted, Acts concentrates.

The letters are usually referred to as a group—the Catholic Epistles. "Catholic" is here used in its basic sense of "universal," referring to the letters as not addressed to a single church or person, as were the Pauline letters. To avoid possible confusion, they are sometimes known as the universal or general epistles. However, that should not detract from the fact that they were written to particular churches, though the probability is that they were soon copied and passed on to other churches. As such they give a fuller picture of early Christian growth and expansion than we receive from a traditional overdependence on Acts and the Pauline letters.

Not least of importance is the information and reminder they provide of the mission and contribution to church foundation and growth which the letter-writers made during the first century. In Christian history, who could name a more significant group? James and Jude, brothers of Jesus himself,[1] and Peter and John, the other two names which, beside Paul and James, resonate most richly in the beginnings of Christianity. It was no doubt this which encouraged whoever took the initiative to collect the written remains of these four to ensure that they were not lost. Other names, like Clement and Ignatius, would soon resonate through the Mediterranean churches, and their writings would be valued highly. But they did not belong to the initial period; they were not founding fathers; they had not belonged to the first group of disciples of Jesus. It was this nearness to Jesus which the second generation of Christianity missed and which made them all the more desirous to preserve whatever writings they could which ensured their own continuity with and faithfulness to the good news which Jesus both brought and embodied.

The Letter of James

The letter begins rather dramatically: "James, a servant of God and of the Lord Jesus Christ, to the twelve tribes in the Dispersion" (Jas 1:1). Since in earliest Christianity the other prominent James, the brother of John, was executed by Herod Agrippa in about 42 CE (Acts 12:2), the only plausible candidate as author of the New Testament letter is James the brother of Jesus. He is mentioned only once in the Gospels (Matt 13:55 // Mark 6:3), but an appearance of the risen Jesus to James was prominent in earliest Christian memory (1 Cor 15:7), and

---

1. Traditional (Roman) Catholic insistence on the (perpetual) virginity of Mary, mother of Jesus, would prefer to call James and Jude "half brothers" or cousins.

he seems to have emerged quite quickly as leader of the believers in Jerusalem itself. In his first visit to Jerusalem after his conversion, Paul mentions seeing only James other than Peter (Gal 1:19). But later on James's leadership role is clear in Acts 12:17, and he in effect chaired the crucial Jerusalem conference deciding what should be expected of gentile converts (Acts 15:13–21; Gal 2:9). His leadership role is confirmed in subsequent references (Gal 2:12; Acts 21:18). All the more interesting, therefore, is it that in the letter attributed to him, nothing is said of that close personal relationship which he had to Jesus. Equally interesting is the fact that the letter is addressed to "the twelve tribes of the diaspora"—"diaspora" denoting the "dispersion" of the Jews from Palestine. This confirms not only that the Pauline mission was reaching round the eastern Mediterranean, but also that Jewish believers in a wide scatter of areas were maintaining a direct connection with the mother church in Jerusalem.

In fact, the letter refers to Jesus on only one other occasion:

My brothers, do you with your acts of favoritism really believe in our glorious Lord Jesus Christ? (Jas 2:1)

And it goes on in a powerful plea to those hearing the letter read to them, that they should respect all who came into their worship gathering, the poor as much as the well-to-do (Jas 2:1–7). That gives us an immediate clue as to how Jesus was remembered in the Jewish diaspora churches and what he was remembered for. It was not so much his death (and resurrection) as the concern he had for the poor which he showed and taught during his ministry. Also relevant here is the fact that, apart from the two references to the "Lord Jesus Christ" already cited, the two references to the hope for "the coming of the Lord" (Jas 5:7, 8), and the advice on anointing the sick with oil "in the name of the Lord" (Jas 5:14–15), the other references to "the Lord" are probably to God.[2] That, of course, is itself of no little interest since it implies that even in what we might refer to as Jesus's own family circle, Jesus could be referred to as "the Lord" in the same way as God was referred to as "the Lord."

2. Jas 1:7, 12; 4:10, 15; 5:4, 10, 11.

It is not at all clear whether this was intended to be a letter written or dictated by James himself. It begins as a letter but does not end as a letter. It may then be that collections or remembrances of James's teaching were put together in a quasi-letter format to be circulated among the Jewish Christian churches. There is an interesting parallel with the Q material, which most scholars see as one of the sources drawn on by Matthew and Luke in composing their Gospels. As we saw (chapter 2 above), the Q tradition could be incorporated into the full Gospel format set out by Mark, and a Q document as such was not retained. But the memory of James's teaching could not be so retained, so we can be grateful that it was encapsulated in this way in a letter format.

The letter itself can be categorized as belonging to the Jewish wisdom literature, well known to us from Proverbs, and the intertestamental Sirach and Wisdom of Solomon. The echoes and occasionally direct quotations particularly from Proverbs and Sirach are frequent.[3] What is interesting is that the letter of James recalls and draws on Jesus's teaching in just the same way, Jesus in effect being recalled as a famous teacher of wisdom, very much in the tradition of Israel's famous wisdom literature. I give examples of the clearest dependency of James on the Jesus tradition, but there any many other echoes of Jesus's teaching.[4]

3. See Dunn, *Beginning from Jerusalem*, vol. 2 of *Christianity in the Making* (Grand Rapids: Eerdmans, 2009), 1133, for details.

4.

JAMES	JESUS	JAMES	JESUS
Jas 1:6	Mark 11:23–24	Jas 4:12	Matt 10:28
Jas 1:11	Mark 4:6	Jas 4:14	Mark 8:36–37
Jas 1:17	Matt 7:11	Jas 4:17	Luke 12:47
Jas 1:22	Matt 7:24, 26 // Luke 8:21	Jas 5:1	Luke 6:24
Jas 1:27	Matt 25:35–40	Jas 5:2	Matt 6:19
Jas 2:10	Matt 5:18–19	Jas 5:5	Luke 16:19, 25
Jas 2:13	Matt 18:28–34; 25:45	Jas 5:7	Mark 4:26–29
Jas 2:14	Matt 7:21	Jas 5:9a	Matt 7:1–2
Jas 2:15–16	Matt 25:35–36	Jas 5:9b	Mark 13:29
Jas 2:19	Mark 1:24; 5:7	Jas 5:10	Matt 5:12
Jas 3:1	Matt 23:8, 10	Jas 5:12	Matt 5:34–37
Jas 3:12	Luke 6:44	Jas 5:14	Mark 6:13
Jas 3:18	Matt 5:9	Jas 5:20	Matt 18:15
Jas 4:10	Luke 14:11		

JAMES	JESUS
Jas 1:5: "If any of you is lacking in wisdom, ask God . . . and it will be given you."	Matt 7:7: "Ask, and it will be given you; search, and you will find."
Jas 2:5: "Has not God chosen the poor in the world . . . to be heirs of the kingdom . . . ?"	Luke 6:20: "Blessed are you who are poor, for yours is the kingdom of God."
Jas 2:8: "You do well if you really fulfill the royal law according to the scripture, 'You shall love your neighbor as yourself.'"	Mark 12:31: "'You shall love your neighbor as yourself.' There is no other commandment greater than these."
Jas 4:9: "Let your laughter be turned into mourning and your joy into dejection."	Matt 5:4: "Blessed are those who mourn, for they shall be comforted."
Jas 4:10: "Humble yourselves before the Lord, and he will exalt you."	Matt 23:12: "All who humble themselves will be exalted."
Jas 5:1: "Come now, you rich people, weep and wail for the miseries that are coming to you."	Luke 6:24: Woe to you that are rich, for you have received your consolation."
Jas 5:2–3: "Your riches have rotted, and your clothes are moth-eaten. Your gold and silver have rusted . . ."	Matt 6:20: "But store up for yourselves treasures in heaven, where neither moth nor rust consumes . . ."
Jas 5:12: ". . . do not swear, either by heaven or by earth or by any other oath, but let your 'Yes' be yes and your 'No' be no, so that you may not fall under condemnation."	Matt 5:34–37: "Do not swear at all, either by heaven . . . or by the earth . . . or by Jerusalem. . . . Let your word be 'Yes, Yes' or 'No, No'; anything more than this comes from the evil one."

Two things are interesting here. One is that the influence of the Jesus tradition is pretty clear. The other is that the teaching of Jesus is not recalled as a fixed tradition which has to be formally attributed. Rather we see that the teaching of Jesus has been absorbed and become in effect an integral part of the Christian paraenesis. It is not the teaching of Jesus respectfully preserved, as it were, in a glass case, to be paraded on special occasions. It is the teaching of *James*, but a teaching which has been impacted, shaped, and molded by the tradition of Israel's wisdom teaching and particularly by the memory of what Jesus taught as part of that tradition—perhaps, indeed, as the climax of that tradition.

So here is the way Jesus was remembered, probably within his own native community and presumably by his own brother. It is the day-to-day practicality of the teaching—not great theological reflection such as we find in Paul and in Hebrews, but practical everyday counsel on how to live a humble and a disciplined life, thoughtful for one's responsibilities and concerned for others. Without James there would be the danger of Christianity being seen as a kind of theological exercise. With James in the New Testament, however, Christians can never forget that they belong to an ancient tradition of Jewish wisdom, and that love of neighbor is as fundamental to the Christian life as any theologizing about Jesus and the creation of humankind.

The (First) Letter of Peter

Somewhat surprisingly, when it comes to the writings which make up the New Testament, 1 Peter is something of a problem. The quality of the Greek makes one wonder whether it was written by a Galilean fisherman; or should we attribute the Greek itself rather to Silvanus, the actual letter-writer (1 Pet 5:12)? The relative lack of personal reminiscence of the life of Jesus, apart from 1 Peter 2:21–25[5] and 5:1, is surprising in a letter attributed to his most famous disciple. So too the strongly Pauline character of the language and contents of the letter is also rather surprising from one whose status in Christian memory is entirely independent of Paul. And the absence of any recollection of Peter

5. The reference is drawn primarily from Isa 53:4–6, 12.

engaged in mission in Asia Minor, apart from the letter itself, is bound to leave us wondering. On the other hand, our knowledge of Peter from the Gospels and Acts is still rather limited, and at the very least the fact that the letter was attributed to Peter reminds us of how highly he was esteemed in earliest Christianity. So whether it was composed or dictated by Peter himself, or used as a way of remembering and celebrating the importance of his role in Christianity's beginnings, may be a discussion which we cannot bring to a clear resolution.

Certainly 1 Peter refers to Jesus far more than does James. The author introduces himself as "an apostle of Jesus Christ" (1 Pet 1:1) and greets his readers as "destined . . . to be sprinkled with his blood" (1 Pet 1:2). He hails "the God and Father of our Lord Jesus Christ" (1 Pet 1:3), with no attempt at a more Trinitarian formulation. He rejoices in the resurrection of Jesus Christ from the dead and draws assurance from the sure hope both of Christ's future revelation (1 Pet 1:3–9) and of the grace which "Jesus Christ will bring you when he is revealed" (1 Pet 1:13). He recalls that his readers were ransomed "with the precious blood of Christ, like that of a lamb without defect or blemish," a destiny determined "before the foundation of the world" but now "revealed at the end of the ages for your sake" (1 Pet 1:18–20). And a strong theme is the extent to which Christ's sufferings can serve as a comfort and reassurance to the recipients in their sufferings: Christ's sufferings leave "an example, so that you should follow in his steps," to which is attached a quotation from Isaiah 53:9 (1 Pet 2:19–23). Those listening to the letter being read could rejoice in that they were sharing in Christ's sufferings (1 Pet 4:13–16).[6]

The extent to which the faith expressed in the letter is focused in Christ is clear from the other references to Jesus in the letter:

1 Pet 2:4–8   "Come to him, a living stone, though rejected by mortals yet chosen and precious in God's sight, and like living stones, let yourselves be built into a spiritual house, to be a holy priesthood,

---

6. See also 1 Pet 1:11; 3:14, 17–18; 4:1, 19; 5:1, 10.

to offer spiritual sacrifices acceptable to God through Jesus Christ"; with further quotations from Isa 28:16, Ps 118:22, and Isa 8:14.

1 Pet 3:18-19   "Christ also suffered for sins once for all, the righteous for the unrighteous, in order to bring you to God. He was put to death in the flesh, but made alive in the spirit, in which also he went and made a proclamation to the spirits in prison" (the disobedient in the days of Noah who perished in the flood); similarly 4:6.

1 Pet 3:21-22   "Baptism . . . now saves you—not as a removal of dirt from the body, but as an appeal to God for a good conscience, through the resurrection of Jesus Christ, who has gone into heaven and is at the right hand of God, with angels, authorities, and powers made subject to him."

1 Pet 4:10-11   Believers must speak and serve "so that God may be glorified in all things through Jesus Christ. To him belong the glory and the power forever and ever. Amen."

The clear sense of Christ as the medium through whom worshipers can draw near to God, whose resurrection is the ground of their confidence and hope, and who preeminently brings glory to God, could hardly be clearer. Also noticeable is the fact that 1 Peter could use the title "Lord" equally for Jesus (1 Pet 1:3; 3:15) and for God (1 Pet 1:25; 3:12), so that the reference in 1 Peter 2:3 and 13 can be taken either way without concern. And the fact that 1 Peter is the only New Testament writing apart from Paul that uses the phrase "in Christ" (1 Pet 3:16; 5:10, 14) should not escape notice. Even more striking is the fact that the letter refers to the Spirit who inspired Israel's prophets as "the Spirit of Christ" (1 Pet 1:11). And it is 1 Peter which includes the thought that between his crucifixion and resurrection Jesus descended into hell to minister there (1 Pet 3:18–19), a rather puzzling reference which was included in the Apostles' Creed but was not retained thereafter.

In dealing with James we listed some notable echoes of the Jesus tradition, wholly understandable if the letter had gathered together memories of James's own exhortations. With 1 Peter we might well have expected the same, but, somewhat surprisingly, while there are echoes, as we see below, there is little that is as close to the Jesus tradition as we saw with James. Does this simply indicate a teaching tradition so well absorbed that much of its distinctiveness has been lost? One would have expected the followers of Jesus to want to make the point that their teaching was drawn directly from Jesus himself. Or were they so conscious of the Lord Jesus's daily risen presence with them that they felt no need to refer back to the specific teaching of his Palestinian ministry? He was still with them, after all, and his earlier teaching was entirely adaptable to their own and differing situations.

At any rate, it is important to note the continuing influence of Jesus and his teaching in a Christianity already well established in Asia Minor. The nearest echoes of the Jesus tradition are as follows:[7]

1 PETER	JESUS TRADITION
1:6; 4:13	Matt 5:12
1:10–12	Matt 13:17
1:17	Luke 11:2
2:12b	Matt 5:16b

7. Other references that may show the influence of the Jesus tradition include:

1 PETER	JESUS TRADITION	1 PETER	JESUS TRADITION
1:8	John 20:29	4:8	Luke 7:47
1:22	John 13:34	4:10	Luke 12:42
1:23	John 3:3	4:14	Matt 5:11
2:7	Mark 12:10	5:5b–6	Luke 14:11
	(Ps 118:22)		
2:17	Mark 12:17		

1 Peter	Jesus Tradition
2:19–20	Luke 6:32 // Matt 5:46–47
3:9, 16	Luke 6:28 // Matt 5:44
3:14	Matt 5:10
4:5	Matt 12:36
4:7	Luke 21:36
4:14	Luke 6:22 // Matt 5:11
5:6	Luke 14:11
5:7	Matt 6:25–34

Particularly noticeable, however, is the elaborated meditation on the significance of Jesus's death (1 Pet 2:21–25). The passage is principally a reflection on the great Servant Song of Isaiah 53, and in the New Testament it is the most powerful expression of the theology which was focused on Isaiah's figure of the suffering servant. It is certainly worth repeating in full:

> Christ also suffered for you, leaving you an example, so that you should follow in his steps. "He committed no sin, and no deceit was found in his mouth" [Isa 53:9]. When he was abused, he did not return abuse; when he suffered, he did not threaten; but he entrusted himself to the one who judges justly. He himself bore our sins [Isa 53:4] in his body on the cross, so that, free from sins, we might live for righteousness; by his wounds you have been healed [Isa 53:5]. For you were going astray like sheep [Isa 53:6], but now you have returned to the shepherd and guardian of your souls. (1 Pet 2:21–25)

Perhaps most striking is the fact that the author of 1 Peter is not particularly acclaimed. As noted above, he introduces himself simply as "an apostle of Jesus Christ" (1 Pet 1:1). And later he exhorts the elders of the communities to which he writes, calling himself "an elder and a witness of the sufferings of Christ" (1 Pet

5:1). But he does not lay claim to any primacy or precedence. All of which, of course, may tell us more both of how Peter himself recalled his ministry and of how he was remembered by those who first cherished his memory and ministry.

1–3 John

The three letters attributed to John clearly belong together and share the distinctively Johannine characteristics of John's Gospel. So it is most natural to take them together. And the letters may give us the clearest indication of who wrote both them and the Gospel. Although 1 John does not indicate its author, both 2 John and 3 John indicate in their opening words that they were written by John "the Elder." How "the Elder" relates to John the apostle remains unclear; this lack of clarity presumably explains why it took some time for the letters to be accepted in the canon of the New Testament.

One of the most interesting questions regarding 1 John in particular is why it was written. The most obvious answer is suggested by 1 John 2:19. There had evidently been something of a schism in the Johannine community. Some had gone out from and left the assembly. And the reason was that they could not, or could no longer, affirm that "Jesus is the Christ." For the author that meant that they denied both the Son and the Father who had sent him (1 John 2:22–23). He condemns them as "antichrist"—the only use of the term in the New Testament (1 John 2:18, 22; 4:3; 2 John 7). The divisive issue was evidently the belief that "Jesus Christ has come in the flesh" (1 John 4:2–3; 2 John 7). The dissenters were presumably of the same mind as those who came to be known as gnostics, who saw a fundamental antithesis between matter and spirit; or, more specifically, docetists, who claimed that Jesus only *seemed* to come in the flesh.[8] For them a real incarnation, a coming from heaven "in the flesh," was actually impossible. So they deduced that Christ, the heavenly Savior, could only have

8. See chapter 3, note 9.

appeared to be in the flesh, his humanity only a seeming humanity. It was this that the Gospel had so resolutely contested: "the Word *became* flesh" (John 1:14). And it was the same battle, now intensified, in which the Johannine epistles were also engaged.[9]

To meet the challenge the author suggests a number of "tests of life" by which the community could discern who truly belonged to their number: particularly the indwelling Spirit,[10] love,[11] obedience,[12] and right confession.[13] Apart from the centrality of reaffirming the incarnation, the more traditional beliefs are reaffirmed:

1 John 1:7   "The blood of Jesus . . . cleanses us from all sin."

1 John 3:5   "He was revealed to take away sins, and in him there is no sin."

1 John 3:16   "We know love by this, that he laid down his life for us."

1 John 4:9   "God sent his only Son into the world so that we might live through him."

1 John 5:6   "This is the one who came by water and blood, Jesus Christ."

But 1 John adds further emphases:

1 John 2:1   "If anyone does sin, we have an advocate with the Father, Jesus Christ."

---

9. Ignatius, writing to churches in Asia Minor, probably not very long after the Johannine epistles were written, fought the same battle (*To the Ephesians* 7; *To the Trallians* 9–10; *To the Smyrnaeans* 1–3).

10. 1 John 3:24; 4:1–3; 4:13; 5:6, 8.

11. 1 John 2:5; 3:16–17; 4:7–12, 17–18.

12. 1 John does not use the term "obey" and prefers to speak of "keeping his commandments" (2:3–4; 3:22, 24; 5:3).

13. 1 John 4:2–3, 15; 2 John 7.

1 John 3:2	"When he is revealed, we will be like him, for we will see him as he is."

1 John 3:8	"The Son of God was revealed for this purpose, to destroy the works of the devil."

As already noted, it was a fundamental belief for the Johannine community that Jesus was the long-expected Messiah/Christ.[14] But more important for the community, as could be expected from the Gospel, was the reference to Jesus as God's Son. For example:

1 John 1:3	"Truly our fellowship is with the Father and with his Son Jesus Christ."

1 John 1:7	"The blood of Jesus his Son cleanses us from all sin."

1 John 2:23–24	"No one who denies the Son has the Father; everyone who confesses the Son has the Father also. . . . If what you heard from the beginning abides in you, then you will abide in the Son and in the Father."

1 John 4:10	"In this is love, not that we loved God but that he loved us and sent his Son to be the atoning sacrifice for our sins."

1 John 4:14–15	"We have seen and do testify that the Father has sent his Son as the Savior of the world. God abides in those who confess that Jesus is the Son of God, and they abide in God."

1 John 5:5	"Who is it that conquers the world but the one who believes that Jesus is the Son of God?"

14. 1 John 1:3; 2:1, 22; 3:23; 4:2; 5:1, 6, 20; 2 John 3, 7, 9.

1 John 5:11–12	"This is the testimony: God gave us eternal life, and this life is in his Son. Whoever has the Son has life; whoever does not have the Son of God does not have life."

2 John 9	"Whoever abides in the teaching of Christ has both the Father and the Son."

A striking feature of 1 John in particular is the development of the theme of abiding in Christ, earlier elaborated in John 15. It was evidently a cherished theme in the Johannine community, and the writer does not hesitate to press home its importance. The goal is that they might "abide" in Christ—for example:

1 John 2:6	"Whoever says, 'I abide in him,' ought to walk just as he walked."

1 John 2:24	"If what you heard from the beginning abides in you, then you will abide in the Son and in the Father."

1 John 3:24	"All who obey his commandments abide in him, and he abides in them."

1 John 4:16	"God is love, and those who abide in love abide in God, and God abides in them."[15]

One of the most striking features of 1 John's Christology is that the author takes the theme of the Spirit promised by Christ in the Gospel, as the *Paraclete*, the promised "mediator" or "intercessor,"[16] and applies it to Christ himself. "If anyone does sin, we have an advocate [*paraklētos*] with the Father, Jesus Christ the righteous" (1 John 2:1), the Paraclete in heaven coordinating with the Paraclete in their midst.

---

15. See also 2:10, 14, 27, 28; 3:6, 9, 17; 4:12, 13, 15, 16; 2 John 9.
16. John 14:16, 26; 15:26; 16:7.

The Johannine letters naturally have many echoes of the Gospel of John. But more interesting are the echoes of the synoptic tradition. The concern about the possibility of being entrapped or "stumbling" (1 John 2:10) may well echo Jesus's teaching in Matthew 18:7. "Those who do the will of God" (1 John 2:17) may well draw on Jesus's teaching preserved in Matthew 7:21. 1 John 2:28 seems to echo Mark 8:38. 1 John 3:4 reflects the concern about "lawlessness" (*anomia*) so prominent in (and distinctive of) Matthew.[17] And 1 John 4:1 shares the concern, again particularly of Matthew,[18] about the danger of false prophets misleading the followers of Jesus. In other words, the Johannine letters confirm that the distinctive Johannine way of remembering Jesus was rooted in the less expansive memories of the synoptic evangelists. That the echoes are most often of the (sometimes also distinctive) Matthean memory of Jesus's teaching simply confirms that Matthew was the most-used version of the ministry and teaching of Jesus in the second century. In other cases the echoes are fainter.[19] But that again may simply remind us that the teaching of Jesus was not retained in strictly controlled formulation but was evidently reflected on, elaborated, and applied in the changing situations of the early Christian communities. The Synoptic Gospels show that Jesus was not remembered in a static, closely restricted way, but in constant engagement with the changing situations of the evangelists themselves and of the churches for whom they wrote. The Gospel of John shows how much the Jesus tradition could be reshaped to meet ever new challenges and opportunities. And 1–3 John confirm how that living memory of Jesus could inform and instruct on how to respond to such challenges and opportunities.

---

17. Matt 7:23; 13:41; 23:28; 24:12.

18. Matt 7:15; 24:11; 24:24.

19. E.g., 1 John 2:18 (Mark 13:6-7, 22-23); 1 John 2:22-23 (Luke 12:8-10); 1 John 3:3 (Matt 5:8); 1 John 3:15 (Matt 5:21-22); 1 John 3:22 (Luke 11:9-10); 1 John 4:11 (Matt 18:32-33); 1 John 4:17 (Matt 10:15); 1 John 5:15 (Matt 21:22); 1 John 5:16 (Matt 12:31a); 2 John 7 (Matt 24:4-5); 2 John 10 (Matt 10:13-14).

Jude and 2 Peter

We take Jude and 2 Peter together, since a comparison of the two letters strongly suggests that one was drawing on the other.[20] Most commentators conclude that 2 Peter was drawing on Jude and should probably be regarded as the last of the NT documents to be written.

Jude

Jude claims to be written by Jude, "brother of James" (Jude 1). The only obvious "James" is again the brother of Jesus, who, as noted above, became leader of the mother church in Jerusalem in the middle of the first century. And Mark 6:3 tells us that Jesus had four brothers, including James and Judas. It is striking that Jude introduces himself in this way, rather than by claiming Jesus as his brother. It may, of course, simply suggest a degree of humility on Jude's part as well as indicating the stature of James in the earliest Christian communities. 1 Corinthians 9:5 suggests that "the brothers of the Lord" were active in missionary work, and it is quite possible that Jude's preaching or teaching was gathered together in letter form out of respect for him. The sequence of warning examples drawn from Jewish history (Jude 5–23) certainly recalls a very distinctive Jewish teacher.

Rather differently from James, Jude refers to Jesus six times, introducing himself as "a servant of Jesus Christ" (Jude 1), and referring to Jesus regularly as "our Lord" (Jude 17, 21, 25), but also as "our only Master and Lord" (Jude 4). In contrast, however, Jude shows few echoes of Jesus's teaching. The most evident are:

Jude 4   Warning example of those who deny Christ (cf. Matt 10:33)

20. Cf. Jude 6–8 (2 Pet 2:4–10); Jude 12–16 (2 Pet 2:17–18); and Jude 17–18 (2 Pet 3:1–3).

Jude 7	Warning examples of Sodom and Gomorrah (cf. Matt 10:15)
Jude 14	The Lord/Son of Man coming in judgment (cf. Matt 25:31)
Jude 15	Judgment on careless speech (cf. Matt 12:36)

It is hard to escape the impression that while Jude certainly was to the fore in affirming and living out of the Lordship of Christ, he drew his distinctive teaching and exhortations more naturally from Israel's history than from Jesus's distinctive teaching.

2 Peter

The consensus view of New Testament scholars is that 2 Peter was not written by Peter. Two features indicate the lateness of the perspective. One is that the delay of the parousia (the second coming of Christ) has, for the first time in the New Testament, become a problem (2 Pet 3:3–12). The other is that Paul's letters have become regarded as Scripture (2 Pet 3:15–16), a status elsewhere not attributed to them prior to the second century. 2 Peter's dependence on Jude, its differences from 1 Peter, and the indications just mentioned of a later perspective all suggest a later attempt to gather and preserve teaching that could be attributed to Peter and was held in sufficient esteem to be preserved and used as a resource for teaching into the second century.

Notably, Jesus is referred to regularly as "our Lord Jesus Christ" (2 Pet 1:2, 8, 14, 16) or "our Lord and Savior Jesus Christ" (2 Pet 1:11; 2:20; 3:18). And, rather strikingly, the letter opens with a reference to "the righteousness of our God and Savior Jesus Christ" (2 Pet 1:1). The writer seems quite ready to refer to the climax of history as "the day of the Lord" (2 Pet 3:10) and as "the day of God" (2 Pet 3:12). But echoes of Jesus's teaching are quite faint. Most notable are probably:

2 Pet 1:8	Mark 4:19
2 Pet 1:14	John 21:18
2 Pet 2:1	Mark 13:22
2 Pet 2:6	Matt 10:15

Particularly noteworthy is 2 Peter 1:14 with its strong allusion to John 21:18–19, itself a distinctively Johannine appendix to John's Gospel forecasting Peter's martyrdom. Also noteworthy is the strong affirmation of 2 Peter 1:16–18 that "we have been eyewitnesses of his majesty," with direct allusion to witnessing Jesus's transfiguration on the mountain (Matt 17:5). Overall, however, it is difficult to escape the sense that the memory of Jesus's ministry has become rather distant, and the relevance of his remembered teaching to the different situations now confronting writer and recipients has become less of a concern. Jesus is still remembered, as 2 Peter 1:16–18 in particular makes most clear, but the degree of dependency on his remembered teaching is quite remote as compared with James and even Paul. The question of how much Christianity would have lost if Jude and 2 Peter had not been included in the New Testament canon invites a somewhat embarrassing answer.

* * *

In a New Testament dominated by the Gospels and the letters of Paul it is easy to overlook the value of the Catholic Epistles. Even in churches that read three or four Bible passages every Sunday, the readings from James, Peter, John, and Jude rarely feature in the subsequent sermon or meditation. But they are an important reminder of the breadth and depth of the founding generation of Christianity. Without them we would have a far more limited appreciation of the impact made by Jesus and of the diverse ways in which his life and ministry, his death and resurrection were remembered and provided a resource for living, for witness, and for ministry. Even when relatively neglected by today's churches, they represent and embody a rich diversity that was Christianity from the first, and without regular engagement with them today's Christianity would be much impoverished.

CHAPTER NINE

Jesus according to

Revelation

T he English title "Revelation" is a direct translation of the
Greek term "apocalypse," denoting the unveiling of heavenly secrets. An apocalypse can be described as crisis literature—a response to crisis when other hope has gone, when,
without direct intervention from heaven, there is little hope for
the future. This is how the literature was born, notably with the
book of Daniel, born of the crisis of Jews exiled in Babylon after
the initial destruction of Jerusalem. And the despair caused by
the subsequent destruction of Jerusalem and its temple in 70 CE
found notable expression in the visions recorded in 4 Ezra. Revelation can be lumped with the latter, when the catastrophe of what
had happened to the earthly Jerusalem could find an answer only
in heaven and in the fuller purpose of God. A not insignificant
fact is that this is the only post-70 New Testament writing which
indicates that the events of 70 CE were experienced by Christians
as equally catastrophic as they certainly were for Israel and Jews.
Somewhat ironically, the Jewishness of Christianity is as clear in
Revelation as it is anywhere else in the earliest decades of Christianity's existence.

The author has no hesitation in claiming that he was inspired and that what he wrote was divinely revealed. He names
himself "John" (Rev 1:1, 4; 22:8). Who this "John" was is not at
all clear. He claims to be a sharer in persecution suffered by his

brothers, and apparently he had been exiled to or imprisoned on the island of Patmos "because of the word of God and the testimony of Jesus" (Rev 1:9). Later he refers to those slaughtered for their testimony (Rev 6:9; 20:4), so the situation envisaged is dark and the author's use of the apocalypse genre wholly understandable. Since persecution of Christians in Asia[1] seems to have increased under the later years of the emperor Domitian's reign (81–96), it suggests a date for Revelation late in the first century.

The Exalted Jesus

The Christology of Revelation is somewhat surprising, though not when we recall the apocalyptic character of Revelation. The writing is introduced as "the revelation of Jesus Christ" (Rev 1:1). The writer, John, records "the testimony of Jesus Christ," a favorite phrase with John,[2] including testimony "to all that he saw" (Rev 1:2). The introductory blessing is "from him who is and who was and who is to come,[3] and from the seven spirits who are before his throne, and from Jesus Christ, the faithful witness, the firstborn of the dead, and the ruler of the kings of the earth" (Rev 1:4–5). This ease with which John refers to Jesus and God in similar language is a feature of his writing. The first hymnic passage (Rev 1:7) echoes Daniel 7:13 ("he is coming with the clouds") and Zechariah 12:10 ("every eye will see him, even those who pierced him"). And John is the only New Testament writer apart from the evangelists to refer Daniel's vision of "one like a son of man" (Dan 7:13) to Jesus (Rev 1:13; 14:14). Nor should we miss the powerful self-revelation of Christ which introduces the letters to the seven churches: "I am the first and the last, and the living one. I was dead, and see, I am alive forever and ever; and I have the keys of Death and of Hades" (Rev 1:17–18).

---

1. "Asia" then was the term for today's western Turkey.
2. Rev 1:2, 9; 12:17; 19:10; 20:4.
3. The same phrase is used of God in 1:8 and 4:8.

Preceding that, the vision of Revelation 1:12–16, of Jesus "with a *golden sash* across his chest . . . *his head and his hair . . . white as white wool, white as snow; his eyes . . . like a flame of fire*, his feet . . . *like burnished bronze* . . . and his voice . . . *like the sound of many waters*," draws on the apocalyptic tradition within Judaism where the glorious angel who appears can be almost identified with God. The echoes of the visions of Daniel (7:9, 13) and Ezekiel (1:24–27; 8:2), indicated by the italicized words, are no doubt deliberate. What is striking is the contrast with such apocalyptic tradition at this point. For example, in the Apocalypse of Abraham 17:2 and the Ascension of Isaiah 8:4–5, the glorious angel refuses worship or to be addressed as "my Lord." And, not surprisingly, Revelation follows the same tradition in regard to the interpreting angel, as is clear particularly in Revelation 19:10 and 22:8–9. In striking contrast, however, Jesus is more clearly worshiped in Revelation than anywhere else in the New Testament. The hymns to the Lamb in chapter 5 are no different in character from the hymns to God in chapter 4. And in passages such as Revelation 5:13 and 7:10 the Lamb is linked with God in a common ascription of adoration:

Rev 5:13   "To the one seated on the throne and to the Lamb be blessing and honor and glory and might."

Rev 7:10   "Salvation belongs to our God who is seated on the throne, and to the Lamb!"

In other words, the inhibitions about worshiping a glorious interpreting angel, which John shared with his fellow apocalyptists, he abandoned in the case of the exalted Christ, the Lamb of God.

This clearly implies that the seer's running together of the descriptions in Ezekiel and Daniel, of God as seen in vision and of glorious angels, was no accident. His intention was precisely to say that the exalted Jesus was *not* merely a glorious angel or to be confused with one. The glorious angel was not to be worshiped. But the exalted Christ was! This is of a piece with the fact, again no doubt deliberate on John's part, that both God and the exalted Christ say, "I am the Alpha and the Omega."[4] Nor does John hold back from referring to the exalted Christ as "the holy one,"[5] knowing full well that "the holy one" is used frequently of God in the LXX, the Greek translation of the Hebrew Old Testament, often in the expression "the Holy One of Israel."[6] Similarly with his affirmation of Jesus as "King of kings and Lord of lords" (Rev 17:14, 19:16), a title presumably fitting for God alone. And some of the descriptions of the exalted Christ's relation to the throne in the seer's vision seem to imply that the Lamb was sitting on *God's* throne (Rev 3:21; 7:17); it is "the throne of God and of the Lamb" (Rev 22:1, 3). This should probably be seen as one of John's ways of acknowledging the fullest significance and status of Christ in relation to God without abandoning his more traditional monotheism. To do so without diminishing the glory of the one God was possible within an apocalyptic tradition as nowhere else, since that tradition was quite familiar with angelic agents of God who embodied the person, majesty, and authority of God.

The title "Lord" is used mostly of God, with only a few references to Jesus.[7] The references to Jesus as "Son of God" are even fewer (Rev 2:18; cf. 12:5), something unexpected in a Johannine document. After the opening verses the references to "Christ" are almost as sparing,[8] including the thought of God and "his Christ" (Rev 11:15; 12:10) and of the saints reigning with Christ (Rev 20:4, 6). The other principal ways of referring to Christ are also manifestly derived from Jewish imagery and usage. Christ as "the Lion of the tribe of Judah" (Rev 5:5) alludes to Genesis 49:9, and Christ as "the Root of David" (Rev 5:5; 22:16) is an allusion to Isaiah 11:1, 10, both indicating that for John the apocalyptic significance of Christ is as the expression of Judah at its best and as the fulfillment of Israel's messianic hopes. The familiar early Christian thought of

---

4. Rev 1:8; 21:6; 22:13.

5. Rev 3:7; cf. 6:10.

6. The phrase occurs twenty-nine times in Isaiah alone and is used of God in Rev 15:4 and 16:5.

7. Rev 11:8; 14:13; 17:14; 19:16; 22:20, 21.

8. Rev 1:1, 2, 5; 11:15; 12:10; 20:4, 6.

Christ as exalted to heaven, ruling with God (Ps 110:1) and sitting in judgment, is taken for granted. And the predictions of catastrophic suffering for believers climax with the reassurance of the heavenly praise, that "the kingdom of the world has become the kingdom of our Lord and of his Christ, and he will reign forever and ever" (Rev 11:15). As should not be surprising in apocalyptic literature, in Revelation the Christology is never straightforward or simple.

Other distinctive features of Revelation's portrayal of Jesus include the curious reflection on the tribulations of the church depicted as the mother of Christ (Rev 12); the rather Johannine reference to Christ as "the Word of God" (Rev 19:13); the thousand-year reign of the martyred saints with Christ following "the first resurrection" (Rev 20:4, 6); "the new Jerusalem, coming down out of heaven . . . , prepared as a bride adorned for her husband" (Rev 21:2), that is, the Lamb (Rev 21:9); and the concluding reassurance: "See, I am coming soon!" (Rev 22:7).

The Letters to the Churches

The letters to the seven churches of Asia are dictated by Christ and addressed "to the angel of" each church, represented by a star, while each church is represented by a golden candlestick (Rev 1:20). Each letter is introduced with the formula: "These are the words of . . . ," followed by a reference to Christ distinctive of each church:

Ephesus: "Him who holds the seven stars in his right hand, who walks among the seven golden lampstands" (Rev 2:1).

Smyrna: "The first and the last, who was dead and came to life" (Rev 2:8).

Pergamum: "Him who has the sharp two-edged sword" (Rev 2:12).

Thyatira:	"The Son of God, who has eyes like a flame of fire, and whose feet are like burnished bronze" (Rev 2:18).
Sardis:	"Him who has the seven spirits of God and the seven stars" (Rev 3:1).
Philadelphia:	"The holy one, the true one, who has the key of David, who opens and no one will shut, who shuts and no one opens" (Rev 3:7).
Laodicea:	"The Amen, the faithful and true witness, the beginning/origin of God's creation" (Rev 3:14).

The first four descriptions of Christ recall elements of the description of the "one like a Son of Man" who appeared to John in 1:12–18. The latter three are more distinctive—attributing to Christ "the seven spirits of God" (Rev 3:1) and "the key of David."[9] Highly distinctive is the designation of Christ as "the Amen" (Rev 3:14), a designation which appears only here in the New Testament.[10] And Christ is evidently the model for the "faithful witness" (Rev 1:5; 2:13), a witness-bearing role which John exemplified (Rev 1:2, 9) and which he encourages from start to finish.[11]

Equally distinctive are the judgments made by the one who dictates the letters, and the power and authority which they claim. The church of *Ephesus* is warned that their lampstand could be removed unless they repent, but Christ promises to those who conquer that they will be permitted "to eat from the tree of life that is in the paradise of God" (Rev 2:7). The church of *Smyrna* is encouraged in the face of "the slander on the part of those who say they are Jews and are not, but are a synagogue of Satan" (Rev 2:9)—an astonishing condemnation arising from the tensions between Jews

9. Rev 3:7; cf. 5:5; 22:16.
10. There is probably an allusion to Isa 65:16, where a literal translation would read "he shall bless by the God of Amen."
11. Rev 6:9; 11:7; 12:11, 17; 19:10; 20:4.

and Jesus believers in Asia Minor. They are promised "the crown of life" and that they "will not be harmed by the second death" (Rev 2:10–11). The church of *Pergamum* is sternly warned against false teaching and is promised: "To everyone who conquers I will give some of the hidden manna, and I will give a white stone, and on the white stone is written a new name that no one knows except the one who receives it" (Rev 2:17). These words are a mysterious but strangely comforting reassurance. The most fearsome condemnation is made of the church of *Thyatira*, who "tolerate" the false teaching of a prophet (Jezebel), but with encouragement to those who have resisted "the deep things [teachings] of Satan." The promise to those who conquer is that they will be given "the morning star," presumably a promise that they will have part in the messianic triumph of Christ indicated in Revelation 22:16.

Almost as fearsome is the condemnation of the church in *Sardis*. To the few "who have not soiled their clothes" Christ promises that they "will walk with me, dressed in white"; "I will not blot your name out of the book of life; I will confess your name before my Father and before his angels" (Rev 3:4–5). The church in *Philadelphia* is given the greatest commendation: "you have but little power, and yet you have kept my word and have not denied my name" (Rev 3:8). Intriguing is once again the condemnation of local Jews—"those of the synagogue of Satan who say that they are Jews and are not, but are lying" (Rev 3:9)—a further indication of a devastating breakdown in relations between new churches in Asia Minor and the much longer established synagogues. Notably the promise of Christ's soon coming is strongly affirmed, as in the climax of the writing (Rev 22:20). And, ironically in view of the breakdown of relations with local synagogues, and intriguingly for his status, the exalted Christ promises to make the Philadelphian believers "a pillar in the temple of my God. . . . I will write on you the name of my God, and the name of the city of my God, the new Jerusalem that comes down from my God out of heaven, and my own new name" (Rev 3:12). A notable feature is Jesus's fourfold reference to "my God." The author evidently had no embarrassment in the range of ways he speaks of the relation between Jesus and God.

The criticism of the church of *Laodicea* is also rather devastating, not least because it focuses on the "lukewarmness" of the Laodiceans and their failure to realize their own (spiritual) poverty (Rev 3:16–17). The accompanying invitation is one of the most famous and most moving:

> Listen! I am standing at the door, knocking; if you hear my voice and open the door, I will come in to you and eat with you, and you with me. To the one who conquers I will give a place with me on my throne, just as I myself conquered and sat down with my Father on his throne. (Rev 3:20–21)

In a document which exalts Christ so powerfully, we are reminded that probably we should not make too much of Revelation's portrayal of Jesus sharing the throne of God, since the conquering saints are also to be given a place on the heavenly throne. The Christology of the letters of Revelation is one of the writing's most intriguing features.

The Lamb of God

The most strikingly distinctive and prominent feature of Revelation's portrayal of Jesus, however, is the twenty-eight references to Jesus as a "lamb" (*arnion*). So expressive of Revelation's view of Christ is John's treatment at this point, that it is important to have a clear grasp of his presentation of the Lamb and of its christological implications. In particular:

Rev 5:6	"I saw . . . among the elders a Lamb standing as if it had been slaughtered, having seven horns and seven eyes, which are the seven spirits of God sent out into all the earth."
Rev 5:12	The heavenly host sing with full voice, "Worthy is the Lamb that was slaughtered to receive power and wealth and wisdom and might and honor and glory and blessing!"

Rev 6:1   "I saw the Lamb open one of the seven seals . . ."
               on the scroll which foretells the future.

Rev 7:14   The persecuted saints "have washed their robes
               and made them white in the blood of the Lamb."

Rev 7:17   "The Lamb at the center of the throne will be their
               shepherd."

Rev 12:11   "They have conquered him [Satan] by the blood
               of the Lamb."

Rev 13:8   "The book of life of the Lamb that was slaughtered."

Rev 14:1   "I looked, and there was the Lamb, standing on
               Mount Zion! And with him were one hundred
               forty-four thousand who had his name and his
               Father's name written on their foreheads."

Rev 15:3   The saints who have conquered the beast "sing
               the song of the Lamb."

Rev 17:14   The kings allied to the beast "will make war on
               the Lamb, and the Lamb will conquer them, for
               he is Lord of lords and King of kings."

Rev 19:7, 9   The marriage of the Lamb.

Rev 21:9   The bride, the wife of the Lamb.

Rev 21:14   The twelve foundations of the heavenly Jerusa-
               lem inscribed with the names of the apostles of
               the Lamb.

Rev 21:22–23   "I saw no temple in the city, for its temple is the
               Lord God the Almighty and the Lamb. And the
               city has no need of sun or moon to shine on it,

for the glory of God is its light, and its lamp is the Lamb."

Rev 21:27   "Only those [are in the city] who are written in the Lamb's book of life."

Such animal imagery is familiar in apocalyptic literature, though not usually in reference to a messiah. But as a metaphor for one whose death was seen as a sacrifice—the imagery is introduced in chapter 5, the Lamb "standing as if it had been slaughtered" (Rev 5:6, 12; 13:8)—it was deeply rooted in Israel's sacrificial tradition. The persecuted saints "have washed their robes and made them white in the blood of the Lamb" (Rev 7:14) and have conquered Satan "by the blood of the Lamb" (Rev 12:11). In context, however, it is not the image of a weak victim which emerges. For the Lamb is also described as "having seven horns and seven eyes" (Rev 5:6), "horn" being a familiar symbol of royal power,[12] and the "seven eyes" alluding to Zechariah 4:10, symbolizing divine omniscience. And notably it is the Lamb who takes and opens the scroll which reveals the terrifying future.[13] The choice of *arnion* for "lamb," rather than the more familiar *amnos*, may also indicate that John had in mind the sense "ram" as well, since the Lamb of Revelation shares God's throne, exercises judgment (Rev 6:16), and conquers his enemies (Rev 17:14).[14] By choosing this term and its imagery, John was able to hold together the complex elements of his Christology—the Lamb slaughtered, but the saints cleansed by its blood; but also the Lamb conquering Satan and the latter's allies, and now being praised by the heavenly host. Equally notable is the willingness to express the Spirit of God as the seven eyes of the Lamb. The willingness of John to be so flexible in his portrayal of Christ serves as a warning that formulations attempting to express the relation of Christ to God can easily become too restrictive or imprisoning.

12. As in Dan 7:7–8, 11–12.
13. Rev 5:5, 8; 6:1–17; 8:1.
14. Lambs are used in 1 Enoch 90 as an image for the Maccabeans.

*   *   *

Revelation is a curious book, hard to appreciate when set along-side the other New Testament writings. Two things should be remembered when reading Revelation, or listening to a reading from Revelation, especially when the reader in a worship service introduces the reading as (from) "the word of God."

One is that Revelation can be fairly described as "crisis litera-ture." It was written for churches anticipating or already suffering from persecution by state authorities. This was how apocalyptic literature emerged, from the crises caused by the destruction of Jerusalem and its temple. And Christians, even in Asia Minor in the late first century, shared in that experience of catastrophe and persecution. Nothing else within the New Testament can quite compare with what Revelation envisages. Even the dismay caused by Jesus's crucifixion was quickly replaced by the joy of his resurrection. And nothing that Paul experienced to which he refers in his letters could match what Revelation portrays. Which makes it hard for most twenty-first-century Christians to feel that Revelation was written for them or speaks to them. Jews in the Warsaw ghetto, or prisoners in Japanese prisoner of war camps during the Second World War, or those suffering in the various military catastrophes of the twenty-first century might well find in the Revelation of John some source of hope. But for the ma-jority of those reading Revelation or listening to it being read, how does Revelation speak to them? How does its portrayal of Christ inspire and energize them? Is this simply a New Testament writing to be appreciated for what it tells us about the sufferings of early Christians in Asia Minor, a writing to be held in reserve in case it becomes relevant in some future crisis facing believers in Christ? Crisis literature—retained to remind us of how some early Christians responded to the crises which confronted them, and retained to provide some illustration or guidance on how we could or should respond to future crises? Is that it?

Second, we should certainly be alert to the danger of taking Revelation literally. With almost all the rest of the biblical writ-ings the first rule is that they should be read literally, to take the meaning most obviously intended by the words. But apocalyptic literature emerged because there was no straightforward answer to the crises confronting the authors. They had to turn to symbols and images and metaphors, all of which expressed hope but none of which was intended to be taken literally. Failure to appreciate this distinctiveness of apocalyptic literature has led to too many trying to live as though the world of vision and dream was the real or only world. The key function and character of an apocalypse like the revelation given to John is precisely the attempt to look beyond the immediate world for hope to sustain life when faith is being suppressed in the present world.

And what then should we make of the portrayal of or reference to Christ in the revelation given to John? We should not take it literally, of course. Jesus was not a lamb. The question is rather what the portrayal of Jesus as a lamb signifies within an apocalyptic scenario. Nor should we become concerned about trying to correlate all the different references to Jesus, or to merge them into a single, coherent Christology. It should not be assumed that the images of different visions were intended by the author to be integrated or to be integratable into a single image. The one thing which really matters, in terms of Christology, is that in John's visions Jesus was seen again and again as the key to making sense of the crises confronting the churches and as at the center of the hope for a successful resolution of these crises. It is not the detail that matters—the sometimes confusing details of the various visions—but the fact that Jesus remained at the center of the hope. What matters is that the various crises had not undermined John's faith in Christ. On the contrary, it was when John looked through and beyond these crises, Jesus remained central to the hope and confidence which John expressed. That was the heart of "Jesus according to John"—Jesus as the focus of hope, of sure hope, in the midst of and through whatever crises the present age throws at us.

Jesus according to . . .

What a fascinating sequence of testimonies. All of them indicate how engaging and influential was the figure of Jesus, and how varied was the impact he made on those who became his first disciples and who left us written accounts of that impact made on them by Jesus's brief life, his death, and his resurrection. For Christians, of course, one of the great features of the story of Jesus is that the story is not yet and by no means finished. The impact Jesus initially made in the early first century of the present era continues to exert its influence. Christians today testify more than willingly that the impact of Jesus is not simply a sequence of events in history, and not simply of teaching given twenty centuries ago that has enduring significance and power. There is the continuing impact, Christians believe, and experience, the impact of the living Christ, known in worship and fellowship.

So, as suggested in the preface, it is quite natural to think of the story of Jesus and of the impact made by Jesus as by no means finished. And as the impact in the first century was already quite varied, as indicated in the preceding chapters, so it is easy to imagine that the impact made today will be still more, indeed much more, varied than it was twenty centuries ago. So, why not carry forward the story of Jesus, and the story of "Jesus according to . . ."? Such testimonies will never have the power of the first

(New Testament) stories. But in their own way they will testify to the continuing impact made by the story of Jesus and by the risen Jesus whom Christians still proclaim today.

So, I ask again, how about "Jesus according to you"? Since we are all different—as the New Testament writers were different—our several testimonies will be different too. What a fascinating symphony (and I mean sym-phony) such witness bearing could or would produce. And what a fresh challenge and stimulus might such a symphony give to a generation for most of whom the story of Jesus belongs solely to the past, the distant past. Jesus for today! Jesus according to us! Who's for it?

The Probable Date and Place of Origin for Documents of the New Testament

	Palestine	Syria	Asia	Greece	Rome
50–52				1 & 2 Thessalonians Galatians	
53–55			1 & 2 Corinthians		
56–57				Romans	
60–62					Philippians Colossians Philemon
>62			Ephesians?		
65–75					Mark
75–85	James	Luke–Acts			
85–90		Matthew			
c. 90	Jude		Pastorals Revelation		Hebrews 1 Peter
95–100			John 1–3 John		
110–120					2 Peter

APPENDIX 2

The Life and Mission of Paul

c. 1 BCE–2 CE	Birth in Tarsus
c. 12–26	Education in Jerusalem
31–32	Persecution of Hellenists
32	Conversion
34/35	Flight from Damascus and first visit to Jerusalem
34/35–47/48	Missionary of the church of Antioch
47–48	Jerusalem council and incident at Antioch
49/50–51/52	Mission in Corinth (1 and 2 Thessalonians, Galatians)
51/52	Third visit to Jerusalem and Antioch
52/53–55	Mission in Ephesus (1 and 2 Corinthians)
56/57	Church building in Corinth (Romans)
57	Final trip to Jerusalem and arrest
57–59	Detention in Jerusalem and Caesarea
59	Attempt to sail to Rome
60	Arrival in Rome
60–62	House arrest in Rome (Philippians, Philemon, Colossians?)
62??	Execution

Many scholars believe that Ephesians was written by a close companion of Paul after his death in order to sum up his mission.

Most scholars believe that the Pastoral Letters (to Timothy and Titus) reflect later circumstances and were attempts to indicate how Paul would have responded to later challenges confronting two of the most important people on his mission team.

Bibliography

Dodd, C. H. *The Interpretation of the Fourth Gospel*. Cambridge: Cambridge University Press, 1960.

Dunn, James D. G. *Beginning from Jerusalem*. Vol. 2 of *Christianity in the Making*. Grand Rapids: Eerdmans, 2009.

———. *Christology in the Making*. 2nd ed. Grand Rapids: Eerdmans, 1999.

———. *Jesus Remembered*. Vol. 1 of *Christianity in the Making*. Grand Rapids: Eerdmans, 2003.

———. *The Theology of Paul the Apostle*. Grand Rapids: Eerdmans, 1998.

Ehrman, Bart, trans. *The Apostolic Fathers*. 2 vols. Loeb Classical Library. Cambridge, MA: Harvard University Press, 2003.

Jowett, Benjamin. *Thucydides: Translated into English*. 2 vols. 2nd ed. Oxford: Clarendon, 1900.

Kähler, Martin. *The So-Called Historical Jesus and the Historic Biblical Christ*. Philadelphia: Fortress, 1964.

Meier, John P. *A Marginal Jew: Rethinking the Historical Jesus*. 5 vols. New Haven: Yale University Press, 1991–2016.

Sanders, J. N. *The Fourth Gospel in the Early Church: Its Origin and Influence on Christian Theology up to Irenaeus*. Cambridge: Cambridge University Press, 1943.

Wrede, William. *The Messianic Secret*. Translated by J. C. G. Greig. Cambridge: James Clarke, 1971.

Wright, N. T. *Jesus and the Victory of God*. London: SPCK, 1996.

Index of Subjects

Index of Scripture and Other Ancient Texts